Pacemaker® American Government Third Edition

Reviewers

We thank the following educators, who provided valuable comments
and suggestions during the development of this book:

Pacemaker Curriculum Advisor: Stephen C. Larsen, formerly of the
University of Texas at Austin
Subject Area Consultant: Gerri Cassinelli, Rolling Hills Middle School,
Cupertino, California

Executive Editor: Jane Petlinski
Project Manager: Suzanne Keezer
Project Editor: Renée Beach
Associate Production Editor: Amy Benefiel
Lead Designer: Joan Jacobus
Market Manager: Katie Erezuma
Manufacturing Supervisor: Mark Cirillo
Series Cover Design: Evelyn Bauer

About the Cover

The Constitution created three branches of government. The executive branch is led by the
President and Vice President. The legislative branch is made up of Congress. The judicial branch is
made up of the courts. What images from the cover relate to each branch of government?

ISBN: 0-130-23617-9

Printed in the United States of America
1 2 3 4 5 6 7 8 9 10   04 03 02 01 00

1-800-848-9500
www.globefearon.com

PACEMAKER®

American Government

Globe
Fearon

Upper Saddle River, New Jersey
www.globefearon.com

Contents

Chapter 7   The President and the Executive Branch   82

Chapter 8   Executive Departments and Independent Agencies   98

Chapter 9   The Judicial Branch   116

x

A Note to the Student

The United States Constitution was written in 1781. The system of government it created has stayed the same for more than 200 years. Why should you care about the Constitution and the workings of government? Every day the government makes decisions that have an impact on your life. As a United States citizen, you have the opportunity—and the right—to influence the government as well.

This book will give you a basic understanding of the system of government of the United States. First you will learn about the roots of the government. You will discover that the United States system reflects some principles of government that are thousands of years old. Then you will learn how federal, state, and local governments work, independently and cooperatively, for the good of all citizens. Perhaps most importantly, you will learn about the freedoms and rights guaranteed to all United States citizens.

You will find several study aids in the book. At the beginning of every chapter, you will find **Learning Objectives**. These objectives will help you focus on the important points covered in the chapter. The **Words to Know** section at the beginning of each chapter will give you a preview of the vocabulary you may find challenging. At the end of each chapter, a **Summary** will give you a quick review of what you have just learned.

Also, as you read the chapters, look for the notes in the margins of the pages. The notes are there to make you stop and think. Some notes comment on the material that you are learning, while others extend your learning. Sometimes, the notes remind you of something you already know.

As you read the chapters, pay attention to the special features. The features will help you to gain new skills and introduce you to government issues. You will also find features that will tell you about court cases and how those decisions have affected your rights.

We hope you enjoy reading about the way our government works. Everyone who put this book together worked very hard to make it interesting as well as useful. The rest is up to you. Our success is in your accomplishment.

The Presidents of the United States

	Years in Office		Years in Office
1. George Washington	1789–1797	22. Grover Cleveland	1885–1889
2. John Adams	1797–1801	23. Benjamin Harrison	1889–1893
3. Thomas Jefferson	1801–1809	24. Grover Cleveland	1893–1897
4. James Madison	1809–1817	25. William McKinley**	1897–1901
5. James Monroe	1817–1825	26. Theodore Roosevelt	1901–1909
6. John Quincy Adams	1825–1829	27. William Howard Taft	1909–1913
7. Andrew Jackson	1829–1837	28. Woodrow Wilson	1913–1921
8. Martin Van Buren	1837–1841	29. Warren G. Harding*	1921–1923
9. William Henry Harrison*	1841	30. Calvin Coolidge	1923–1929
10. John Tyler	1841–1845	31. Herbert C. Hoover	1929–1933
11. James K. Polk	1845–1849	32. Franklin D. Roosevelt*	1933–1945
12. Zachary Taylor*	1849–1850	33. Harry S. Truman	1945–1953
13. Millard Fillmore	1850–1853	34. Dwight D. Eisenhower	1953–1961
14. Franklin Pierce	1853–1857	35. John F. Kennedy**	1961–1963
15. James Buchanan	1857–1861	36. Lyndon B. Johnson	1963–1969
16. Abraham Lincoln**	1861–1865	37. Richard M. Nixon***	1969–1974
17. Andrew Johnson	1865–1869	38. Gerald R. Ford	1974–1977
18. Ulysses S. Grant	1869–1877	39. James E. Carter, Jr.	1977–1981
19. Rutherford B. Hayes	1877–1881	40. Ronald Reagan	1981–1989
20. James A. Garfield**	1881	41. George H.W. Bush	1989–1993
21. Chester A. Arthur	1881–1885	42. William J. Clinton	1993–2000

* died in office   ** assassinated while in office   *** resigned while in office

Unit 1

The American Way of Government

Chapter 1

Roots of American Government

Both the Declaration of Independence and the U.S. Constitution were adopted in Philadelphia's Independence Hall.

Learning Objectives

- Explain how the ancient Greeks practiced democracy.
- Explain how the ancient Romans practiced representative democracy.
- Identify the three English ideas of government that became part of the American system of government.

Words to Know

government	the control or organization of a country and its people
constitution	a written set of laws, the rules of a government
democracy	government of a country by its people
republic	a government by which power is held by representatives elected by the people
liberty	freedom
elect	to choose by voting
dictator	person who has complete power to rule over others
representative	a person who is chosen to act or speak for others
veto	the power to forbid or stop an act of government
laws	the body of official rules of a country that must be obeyed
colony	land owned and governed by another country

The Ideas Behind Our Way of Government

Suppose you were asked to describe the American way of **government** in only one word. You might very well use one of the following words: **constitution**, **democracy**, **republic**, **liberty** or freedom.

You have heard the words *liberty* and *republic* in the salute to the American flag. You may have some ideas about what these words mean. However, do you know why they are important to us? Do you know where these ideas for our government came from?

To find out, we must go back in time. The ideas of democracy started in another land more than

2,000 years ago. These ideas were carried on and have been added to in the hundreds of years since then. Many of these ideas about democracy were written into the U.S. Constitution in 1787.

In this chapter you will learn how the ideas of democracy, republic, and liberty came about. Those ideas started long before our country was born.

What Is a Democracy?

Can you remember the first time you voted on something? Perhaps it was at home. Your family voted on whether to have eggs or pancakes or cold cereal for breakfast. Or perhaps you helped **elect** the leaders of a club you belonged to.

Government Skills

HOW TO STUDY YOUR GOVERNMENT BOOK

You can get the most out of studying if you follow a plan.

1. **Look ahead at what you will read.** Read the name of the chapter. Then read the headings in blue print. Look at the pictures and their captions. At the beginning of each chapter is a list of learning objectives. These are the most important points to remember in the chapter. Study them and then look for them in the chapter.

2. **Learn the Words to Know.** Study the words before you begin to read. Ask for help if you need it.

3. **Read and take notes.** Look for the main ideas. The headings in blue print often state them. Try turning the headings into questions. Then write the answers to the questions as you read each section.

4. **Review.** Before you write your answers to the review questions, try answering the questions out loud. Work with a friend. Explain the answers to each other. Review the Words to Know.

Having a vote means having the power to choose. Democracy means "government by the people." In a democracy, the people have the power to choose. Democracy is the most important idea behind the American form of government. The power of our government rests with the people.

Democracy in Ancient Greece

Many ideas in our government have come from governments of the past. Ancient Greece was the first country to practice democracy. The word *democracy* comes from a Greek word. More than 2,500 years ago,

A woman representing the Spirit of Democracy holds up a voting token (close-up at right) in a temple in Athens, Greece.

the people of Greece lived in places called city-states. Each city-state had its own government. The first city-states were ruled by kings. Later, they were ruled by landowners. Some of the landowners became **dictators.** These were rulers with a complete power over the people.

Some dictators ruled fairly and protected the people under their rule. However, others ruled unfairly and selfishly. The people in many city-states wanted a say in their government. To gain this, they removed the dictators from power. Some new governments allowed citizens to vote on the laws. Every adult male could vote on the laws of his city-state. Women, young men, and slaves had no vote.

Some of the Greek ideas are used in American government today. In the United States, all adult men and women can vote.

The Greek city-states were fairly small. When questions of government came up, anyone who had the right to vote could voice his opinion. The United States is too big for that to take place. However, in some places in our country, the people hold town meetings. At these town meetings, the citizens practice the Greek way of democracy. Everyone who wants to speak gets a chance.

✓ **Check Your Understanding**

1. Write one or two sentences describing the meaning of democracy.

2. Name one difference between the way democracy was practiced in ancient Greece and the way it is practiced in the United States today.

Representative Democracy in Ancient Rome

Like the Greeks, the Romans also practiced democracy. However, Rome was a very large city-state. It was too big for everyone to have a direct say on all government questions. So the Romans elected people to represent them in government. This practice is called **representative** democracy. Another name for this kind of government is a republic.

Not all citizens had equal rights. In Rome, as in Greece, only adult, free men could vote. The Romans had two groups, or classes, of men. Rich landowners made up the higher class. The lower class included the workers, farmers, and merchants (sellers of goods).

Every year, the rich landowners elected two men to lead the country. These two leaders could **veto** or forbid each other's decisions. For the government to act, both leaders had to agree. The Romans feared that one leader might try to become a dictator. A dictator might easily forget the well-being of the people.

The Roman leaders shared power with two governing bodies. One was called the *Senate*. It was made up of 300 of the most powerful men in the land. They were chosen by the two leaders to advise them. Once a man became a Senator, he kept that job for life. The other body was called the *assembly*. It was made up of citizens who wrote rules that became Roman **laws**. Members of the assembly also elected the government's two main leaders.

Remember
Where have you heard the words *Senate* and *assembly*? Do you know the names of your state's governing bodies?

Rome's Written Laws

Rome became so big that its laws and rules were written into codes. A code is a collection of rules concerning one subject. The codes had rules to settle fights between citizens. The codes also had rules for carrying out trade. The Romans were not the first people to have written codes. However, their codes became a very large set of laws.

Here are a few ancient Roman laws.

- You can cut down your neighbor's tree if the wind bends it over your land.

- If you hurt you neighbor's arm, you must pay the doctor bill or have your arm cut off.

- You must fix the road in front of your own land. If it is not kept up, then anyone may drive animals and carts across your land.

✓ Check Your Understanding

Were all citizens given the same rights in ancient Rome? Explain your answer.

Today in the United States, we practice many of the Roman ideas of government. We practice a representative democracy by electing our leaders. The leaders make the laws and carry out the work of government.

The Roman idea of veto is a power held by the U.S. President. The President can veto new laws. We also carry on the idea of written laws. The U.S. Constitution is a set of written laws.

The idea of a Senate is also used in our government. We call the U.S. Senate the "upper" house of our elected lawmakers. Like the Romans, we have an "upper" and a "lower" group of lawmakers.

The Senate of ancient Rome advised the leaders who ruled the country.

English Law From the Mother Country

The United States became an independent nation in 1776. Before that, our land was a group of English **colonies**. Many English ideas of law and government became part of the American system of government. This is not surprising. The colonies were under English law for more than 150 years.

Three English ideas of government were kept alive as important parts of an American government.

1. **Law and order** The English had a government for the whole land. They also had town and city governments. They had sheriffs and justices of the peace. Many cities in the United States today still have offices with these same names.

2. **Limits on government** The English believed that the government should not have too much power. They believed that all people have certain rights. Those rights cannot be taken away by governments, dictators, or kings. An old English document called the Magna Carta was based on these ideas. Hundreds of years later, the Bill of Rights was based on these ideas, too.

3. **Representative democracy** The people of England elected representatives to speak for them in the government. The English, too, used the ideas of the Greeks and Romans. They believed that government should serve the people.

The system of government in the United States today is not the same as England's. Many important changes have been made since the U.S. Constitution was written in 1787. However, the United States has kept the same form of government for more than 200 years.

King John signed the Magna Carta in 1215.

LANDMARK CHANGES IN THE LAW
King John Signs the Magna Carta

In the year 1199, a man named John Lackland became king of England. For the next 15 years, John's rule made England's nobles very angry. He treated members of their class very differently than had earlier kings. John forced more of them into military service. He increased their taxes unfairly. His courts decided cases according to his wishes, not according to law.

By the year 1215, the nobles were fed up. They drew up a list of rights they wanted the king to grant them. They knew King John needed their money and service to the country to run his kingdom. However, John refused twice to grant these rights. The nobles then raised an army and forced the king to give in.

In June 1215, King John signed an agreement granting the nobles certain rights. It was called the Magna Carta, or Great Charter. The Magna Carta said that no king could raise taxes without the people's consent. It also promised rights to people charged with breaking the law. It said that people should be "judged by their peers," or equals, and by the law of the land.

At the time, the Magna Carta only granted these rights to England's nobles. However, over a period of time, these rights became part of English law for all the people. More than 500 years later, these ideas became the foundation of the U.S. Constitution and U.S. law.

You Decide

Were the nobles right or wrong to force King John to agree to the Magna Carta? Give at least one reason for your answer.

Summary

The United States has a democratic form of government. American democracy has its roots in the governments of ancient Greece and ancient Rome.

The city-states of ancient Greece practiced democracy. Every adult free male could vote directly on all government matters.

Rome was the first land to become a republic. The Romans elected representatives to help govern them. Rome had two governing bodies that shared power with the two men elected as leaders.

The American colonies took many of their ideas for a government from old English law. The three most important ideas were (1) law and order, (2) limits on government, and (3) representative democracy.

In England, the Magna Carta limited the power of the king. Many of the rights it granted in 1215 became part of the U.S. Constitution more than 500 years later.

elect
constitution
liberty
dictator
democracy

Vocabulary Review

Complete each sentence with a term from the list.

1. In the United States, the citizens _____ the President.

2. A _____ has complete power over others.

3. In a _____, the citizens elect their leaders.

4. A _____ lists the rules of a government of a country.

5. To make their own choices, people must have _____.

Chapter Quiz

Write your answers in complete sentences.

1. In which country was democracy in government first practiced?

2. Which people were the first to practice representative government?

3. What was one of the two governing bodies in ancient Rome?

4. Which groups did *not* have the right to vote in ancient Greece?

5. What is the name of the document that limited the power of the English king?

6. **Critical Thinking** Name at least *two* ways in which the United States today practices the ideas of government of ancient Rome.

7. **Critical Thinking** Would any of the ancient Roman laws be helpful today? Explain your answer.

Write About Government

Complete the following activities.

1. Make a list of the ideas of government the United States borrowed from ancient Greece and ancient Rome.

2. List the three main ideas of government and law the United States used from English law. Describe each idea.

3. In your own words, describe what the Magna Carta promised. Why is it important to the United States?

Chapter 2

Democracy in the Colonies

Representatives, shown here in Virginia, helped make laws in the early American colonies.

Learning Objectives

- Explain how self-government got its start in the colonies.
- Explain the purpose of the Mayflower Compact.
- Describe the ways the Pilgrims practiced direct democracy.
- Explain how the idea of freedom of religion grew in the colonies.
- Describe the actions of the First and Second Continental Congresses.
- Explain the meaning and importance of the Declaration of Independence.

Words to Know

direct democracy	government in which each person in a group votes on all matters
governor (in the colonies)	someone chosen by the king to rule over a colony
contract	written agreement between two or more people
charter	any written statement of rights or permissions granted by a ruler or a government
political	having to do with matters of government

New Government in a New Land

Suppose you were in charge of setting up a new club. What rules and laws would you want to have? Where and when would your club meet?

The first English settlers in North America did not find towns and cities like those they left behind. Many of the old laws would not work in the new land. The colonists had to make new rules to fit their new lives. They set up governments that had to work in the colonies.

The first two English colonies established in America had different experiences with self-government, a system in which people make up their own laws. In Virginia, self-government came slowly, after several years of struggle and unhappiness. When it was established, the representative system resembled the one used in ancient Rome. In Massachusetts, the form of self-government, **direct democracy**, was patterned like that of ancient Greece.

The First Representative Government

The first English settlers to arrive in North America landed in Jamestown, Virginia, in 1607. The colonists were sent by a large English trading company, the London Company. The colonists had agreed to work for the company for seven years. After that, they would be free to work for themselves. The settlers worked hard for several years. However, many of them became unhappy. The reason was that none of the colonists had a say in how they were governed. The company that owned the colony appointed a **governor** who had complete power.

Things remained this way for several years. Then the London Company changed its mind. It decided that the colony would be more successful if the people had a say in their own government. The company allowed the colonists to elect men from each settled district to a governing body. It was called the House of Burgesses. The elected representatives would help make some of the laws for the colony. The House of Burgesses first met on a very hot day in July 1619. That was the start of self-government in America.

Direct Democracy Under the Mayflower Compact

The Pilgrims sailed from England in 1620 on the ship *Mayflower*. They planned to settle in the area controlled by the London Company. A storm blew the *Mayflower* off course. The Pilgrims were beyond the control and rules of the London Company. However, the Pilgrims knew they were still under the rule of the English king. Before they landed, they drew up a **contract.** The contract was a plan for a government. Under this agreement, the Pilgrims promised to join together to make a government for the good of the colony. They promised to make laws and choose

History Fact

A burgess was a free white man, usually a landowner.

leaders. They also promised to obey these laws and the leaders. The Pilgrims' agreement was called the Mayflower Compact.

Soon, there were towns in Massachusetts. Each town's church became the meeting place for government. Each male voted on the government matters that came up. This form of government was a direct democracy, like the city-states of ancient Greece.

✓ **Check Your Understanding**

1. What was the House of Burgesses? Why was it important?

2. Why did the Pilgrims make a contract?

Massachusetts colonists signed the Mayflower Compact before arriving in America.

Starting New Colonies for Religious Freedom

Remember
Each Massachusetts town was a direct democracy. Each male could vote on government matters.

The Massachusetts colonists came to North America to be free to form their own church. However, the settlers' new church and government had many strict rules. One of the rules said that no other churches were allowed in the colony.

Some colonists felt that this was wrong. They wanted to be free to set up any kind of church they wished. They felt the Massachusetts church was behaving no better than the old Church of England.

For this reason, some people left the Massachusetts colony. They set up two new colonies called Connecticut and Rhode Island. In these colonies, the people were free to worship as they wished. Laws would not tell people what kind of church they had to attend. This idea of *religious freedom* later took hold in all 13 colonies. Today, all Americans have the freedom to practice any religion they choose.

The First Written Constitutions

The colonies of Connecticut and Rhode Island were started with **charters** signed by England's king. These charters gave the people freedom to govern themselves. They were allowed to make their own laws. Each town elected leaders and representatives. The people also elected their own governor and judges. Connecticut and Rhode Island also became the first colonies to draw up written constitutions. These documents listed the powers of the government as well as the **political** rights of the people.

Other colonies soon wrote their own constitutions. They took many ideas from the Connecticut and Rhode Island documents. Those ideas were later used in the U.S. Constitution.

Differences Over Colonial Rule

Although they had some self-government, the colonies were still owned and ruled by Great Britain. The governors tried to carry out the wishes of the British king. However, Britain was 3,000 miles away. It took two months for even important news to get across the Atlantic Ocean. So, as time went on, the colonists gained more control of their own governments.

One way they did this was to limit the powers of the king's governors. The elected representatives passed laws to give themselves the "power of the purse." That meant that the lawmakers had final say on all the governors' plans for raising and spending money.

The British government still protected the colonies, however. It sent soldiers to help the colonists fight the French and Indian War. However, as a result of that war, relations between Great Britain and the colonies became worse.

During the 1760s, the British lawmaking body, Parliament, passed new laws that taxed the colonists. Britain and the colonies had won a major victory in the French and Indian War. They had gained much new territory from France. However, fighting the war proved to be very costly. Parliament felt that the colonists should help pay the large debt. After all, the money had been spent for the good of the colonies as well as for Britain.

Even so, every new tax that Parliament passed angered the colonists. They pointed out that they had no power to elect representatives to Parliament. "No taxation without representation!" they cried. "Have we gone back to the dark ages before the Magna Carta?" they asked.

History Fact

In 1707, Scotland and England joined together. The combined nation became known as Great Britain, or Britain.

After the French and Indian War, the British did not allow the colonists to settle much of the new territory gained from France. This was one more British act that angered the colonies.

The colonists felt that their rights were being taken away. Many of them refused to pay the new taxes. So Parliament passed laws to punish them. This only made things worse. The 13 colonies grew more and more unhappy with British rule. Over time, their unhappiness united them.

✓ **Check Your Understanding**

1. Why did some colonists leave Massachusetts? What *idea* did these colonists believe in?

2. How were Connecticut and Rhode Island self-governing colonies? Give at least two examples.

The British Parliament, shown here, passed many acts that angered the colonies—and united them.

The First Continental Congress

In September 1774, representatives from the colonies met in Philadelphia. They came together to talk about their problems with Great Britain and Parliament. This meeting became known as the First Continental Congress.

The representatives to the meeting drew up a Declaration of Rights. It included the colonies' right to self-government and the right to decide their own taxes. It also included the right to manage their own affairs.

The representatives said that Parliament had no right to pass laws on the colonies that were mainly taxes. Only the colonies' own governing bodies could tax the colonists.

The members of the Continental Congress also drew up a *petition* to King George III. It asked him to help stop all the wrongs Parliament had brought on the colonies. If Parliament did not lift these taxes, the colonies would refuse to buy or sell British goods.

Both Parliament and the king refused to act. The only thing they did was to send more of their troops to the colonies. This caused the colonies to begin stocking war supplies. Within six months, fighting broke out between British troops and the colonists.

Government Fact

A *petition* is a written request, usually signed by many people.

The Second Continental Congress

British troops and colonists from Massachusetts fought each other in April 1775. In May, the Second Continental Congress met in Philadelphia. This time, all 13 colonies knew that a full war with Great Britain was almost certain. They decided to form an army of colonists to defend their rights. George Washington was chosen to lead the army.

Less than a year later, the Second Continental Congress decided to break all ties with Great Britain. The colonies would declare themselves a free and independent nation. Thomas Jefferson was asked to write a Declaration of Independence. On July 4, 1776, the Declaration of Independence was accepted by Congress and signed by all its members.

With that, the Second Continental Congress became the first government of the United States of America. It had no constitutional basis. The British government condemned the Congress as an "unlawful assembly." The British also called the group of

The colonies became the United States of America when the Declaration of Independence was signed on July 4, 1776.

delegates a "den of traitors." Yet the Congress continued to exist. It had the support of colonial and public opinion.

The Second Continental Congress was made up of one body. Each colony—or newly formed state—had one vote. Congress both made the laws of the new nation and saw that the laws were carried out. There was no one leader. Committees made up of the delegates ran the country.

The Congress carried on the war for five years. It supplied the army. It borrowed and printed money. It made contracts with other countries. In addition, it drew up the first written plan for a U.S. government after the war was won. The plan was called the Articles of Confederation.

✓ Check Your Understanding

1. What rights did the members of the First Continental Congress include in their Declaration of Rights?

2. What was the reaction of the British to the petition of the First Continental Congress?

3. Why did the colonists call a meeting of the Second Continental Congress?

Government Skills

READING A POLITICAL MAP

Political maps show countries, states, and cities. They show the borders of places. A border is the line where one country, state, or colony ends and another begins.

Look at the map below.

Which colonies are the Middle colonies? Which are the Southern colonies? Which are the New England colonies? Which had the most land?

The first two settlements in the United States are shown on the map. Name them. In which colonies are they located?

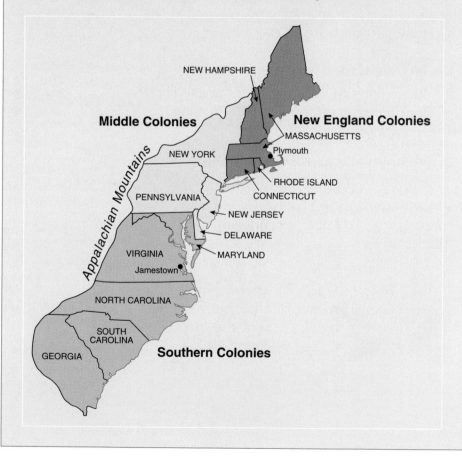

LANDMARK CHANGES IN THE LAW
The Declaration of Independence

The Declaration of Independence is the main document behind the birth of the United States. Its ideas and principles were used to form the U.S. government.

In the document's first part, Thomas Jefferson listed the reasons the colonists were declaring themselves free of Great Britain. They wanted a government that allowed freedom and rights. The document said that all men had certain rights that government could not take away. The most important of these rights were "life, liberty, and the pursuit of happiness." If a government denied these rights to its people, the people had a right to change or abolish that government.

Jefferson then went on to list the reasons why the colonists were against King George III. This part of the document listed 27 charges against the British king. It also stated that because of these charges, the colonists had a right to change their government.

The Declaration of Independence ended by cutting off all the colonies' ties to Great Britain. It stated that all the colonies were free and independent states. It said that they had the power to go to war, make peace, and carry on trade.

The Declaration of Independence clearly stated the thoughts and feelings of a people who really wanted to be free. It stands as one of the most important documents in human history.

You Decide

Were the colonists right or wrong to declare their independence when they did? Why or why not?

Summary

Self-government in the English colonies started in Jamestown, Virginia. In July 1619, an elected body of representatives called the House of Burgesses met for the first time.
The Pilgrims who landed in Massachusetts in 1620 made a contract called the Mayflower Compact. It provided for the colonists to have a say in all matters of government.
Some colonists left Massachusetts because they wanted freedom of religion. They formed the colonies of Connecticut and Rhode Island.
The 13 colonies began to feel that their rights were being taken away by the British Parliament and King George III. In 1774, representatives of the First Continental Congress sent a petition to the king asking for help.
The Second Continental Congress voted to form an army of colonists to defend their rights. In 1776, Thomas Jefferson was asked to write a Declaration of Independence.
The Declaration of Independence declared that all men had certain rights that governments could not take away. It also declared that the colonies had a right to break away from the king's rule.

Vocabulary Review

Write *true* or *false*. If the statement is false, change the underlined term to make it true.

1. A <u>contract</u> dictates the rules of the government.

2. A <u>governor</u> is a chosen ruler.

3. A <u>democracy</u> is ruled by other countries.

4. When something involves the government, it can be described as <u>political</u>.

5. In a <u>direct democracy</u>, citizens participate in every government decision.

Chapter Quiz

Complete numbers 1–5 by filling in the correct
word or phrase. Then answer questions 6 and 7 in
complete sentences.

1. The colonists in Jamestown were granted a form of self-government by _____.

2. The colonists in Massachusetts practiced a form of democracy first practiced in _____.

3. Two colonies formed by people wishing complete religious freedom were _____ and _____.

4. Ideas from the written constitutions of Connecticut and Rhode Island were later used in _____.

5. The colonies' elected representatives limited the powers of the king's governors by giving themselves _____.

6. **Critical Thinking** Why do you think it was necessary for the colonies to go to war against Great Britain in order to get the rights they wanted?

7. **Critical Thinking** Why did the Second Continental Congress write a plan of government?

Write About Government

Complete the following activities.

1. Make a list of the promises that the Pilgrims made to themselves in the Mayflower Compact.

2. After the French and Indian War, problems grew between the colonies and Great Britain. There are two sides to every argument. You are a member of Parliament. Tell why you think the taxes on the colonies are fair. Then take the role of a colonist. Tell why you think Parliament is unfair.

Chapter 3

The Writing of the U.S. Constitution

George Washington spoke to the delegates at the Constitutional Convention.

Learning Objectives

- Identify the five main ideas behind the U.S. and state constitutions.

- Explain how the country's first constitution was too weak to keep lasting peace and safety among the 13 states.

- Outline how the U.S. Constitution was written and passed.

Words to Know

confederation	an agreement of friendship between states
national	having to do with a whole nation or country
trade	the carrying on of business between states or countries
federal government	a form of government with two parts—a national government and state governments
Union	the joining of states into one U.S. government
Constitutional Convention	the meeting in 1787 in Philadelphia to write a new plan for a U.S. government
compromise	the making of an agreement in which each side gives up something
slave	a person who could be bought, sold, and owned by another person
export	any product sent from one country to another for purposes of trade
amendment	change or correction to a written document

Early State Government

Even before the Declaration of Independence was written, many of the colonies had their own constitutions. These constitutions gave power to the people instead of the king. By the end of 1777, most of the states in the newly formed United States had written constitutions.

The state constitutions were not all alike. However, they all shared five main ideas.

1. **Rule by the people** The power of government rests only in the hands of the people.

2. **Limited government** The government must have only a few powers, and they may be decided on and granted only by the people.

3. **Rights and freedoms** All people have certain rights and freedoms that government cannot take away. Seven states had a Bill of Rights written into their constitutions.

4. **Separation of powers** Government was divided into three branches, or parts. One branch had the power to pass laws. Another branch had the power to carry out the laws. The third branch had the power to judge the laws. With this system, the powers of each branch of government were limited.

5. **Checks and balances** Each branch of the government had the power to check, or hold back, the acts of the other branches. These checks helped to balance power between the branches and to limit the power of government.

In 1787, these five ideas became the basic principles of the U.S. Constitution.

Government Fact

After their experience of living under the strong national government of Great Britain, the new states wanted to keep the power for themselves.

The Confederation of States

The new states knew they had to join together as a group in some way. However, they were against a strong government that would have power over the states. The Second Continental Congress wrote a plan for a government of a **confederation** between the states. This plan was called the Articles of Confederation.

It was ratified, or approved, by the states in 1781. That set up the first **national** government of the United States.

Under the Articles, the states would be a group of "friends" working together. The loose government between them would keep the peace and keep them safe. Representatives were sent to a congress, and each state had one vote. Congress itself had just a few important powers. It could make war and peace. It could deal with other countries. It could borrow money or help the states do business with other countries. It could ask the states for money or soldiers.

However, the new Congress had no power to tax the states. Although Congress had power to pass laws, it had no power to carry them out. It also had no power to make rules about **trade** between the states.

These limits on the national government soon caused problems. The states began to act like 13 separate small countries. Some began to print their own money. Many states put taxes on food or goods that came into their states. This made enemies of other states. All the states set up their own armies, and many set up their own navies.

Congress owed large amounts of money that had been borrowed to pay for the war. Even the soldiers who fought in the war had not yet been paid. However, Congress did not have any money, or any real power to raise it. Problems were also widespread in the states. U.S. money had little worth. Many farmers and store owners lost their businesses. Angry farmers and other businessmen who lost money took up arms against their own state governments.

Finally, it became clear that the government under the Articles was too weak. Something had to be done. In 1787, Congress sent a letter to all the states. The

History Fact

George Washington was not happy about the way the states acted toward one another. He wrote, "... we are one nation today, and thirteen tomorrow."

letter asked them to send representatives to a meeting in Philadelphia. The letter explained some changes in government had to be made. The **federal government** had to have more powers. If not, the **Union** would surely come to an end.

✓ **Check Your Understanding**

1. List four powers that Congress had under the Articles of Confederation.

2. What do you think was the greatest weakness of the federal government under the Articles of Confederation? Why was this a problem?

The Constitutional Convention

All the states except Rhode Island sent delegates to the meeting in Philadelphia. The convention began with the idea of making some changes in the Articles of Confederation. Very soon, that idea changed. The Articles were too weak and had too many faults. The delegates decided to write a brand new national constitution. As a result, the meeting in Philadelphia became known as the **Constitutional Convention.**

Government Fact

A *delegate* to a meeting or convention is the same as a representative.

Benjamin Franklin provided advice to the delegates at the Constitutional Convention.

The delegates agreed on the main ideas for a new federal government. They agreed it should have three branches. The new government needed power to make laws. It also needed the power to carry out and judge the laws. In addition, it had to have the power to raise money to do its work.

However, the delegates could not agree on how to set up each branch of the new government. The large states wanted to have more votes in Congress than the smaller states. Smaller states wanted all states to have equal votes. Arguments between the large and small states ran long into the night.

Each side had to give in on some points. In the end, the delegates made several **compromises**. Some truly great new ideas took shape. These were written into the Constitution and have survived to the present day.

Remember
In this system of dividing a government into three branches, no one branch has more power than another.

Compromises Made at the Convention

1. **The Great Compromise** How many representatives should each state have in Congress? The large and small states fought fiercely on this question. The compromise they reached was the plan we have today. The federal government has *two* houses of Congress. All states have two equal votes in the Senate. Votes in the House of Representatives are based on the population of each state. Larger states have more votes.

2. **The Three-Fifths Compromise** The southern states wanted to count their many **slaves** in order to get more seats in Congress. The northern states were against counting slaves as part of a state's population. Finally, they agreed to count three-fifths of the slave population in a state. The number of representatives was balanced between North and South. However,

the South also had to pay for three-fifths of their slaves when federal taxes were placed on all people.

3. **The slave trade compromise** All states agreed that Congress needed the power to make rules on trade. Yet the southern states were afraid that Congress would end the slave trade. They were also afraid that Congress would tax **exports**, products that one country sells to other countries. Tobacco from the southern states was the leading export of the whole country. If Congress taxed exports, the southern states would have to pay the most tax. In the end, the states compromised. The federal government had full power to make rules of trade. However, under the compromise, Congress could not end the slave trade for at least 20 years.

The Debate For or Against the Constitution

The Constitution was finally written. It set up a representative government with three branches. It was based on the same important ideas as the state constitutions that came before it. However, a whole new test began. Before it became law, the Constitution had to be ratified, or accepted, by at least nine states.

The American people were divided into two groups of thought about the Constitution. The *Federalists* liked the Constitution with its strong national government. They felt the Constitution created many federal powers but still left many powers to the states. This group was made up of mostly professional people—lawyers, doctors, and ministers. Wealthy merchants and newspaper owners were also in favor of ratifying the Constitution.

The *anti-Federalists* were afraid that the new Constitution went too far in taking power away from the states. They were afraid the rights of the people

James Madison was the leading contributor to the writing of the Constitution. Later, as one of the authors of The Federalist Papers, *he argued strongly for its ratification.*

might be taken away as well. The anti-Federalists were mostly farmers, small-business owners, and townspeople.

The debate about ratification went on for weeks throughout the country. The Federalists defended their position in a series of newspaper articles. James Madison, Alexander Hamilton, and John Jay carefully explained what had been done in Philadelphia and why. These famous articles are known today as *The Federalist Papers*.

In December 1787, Delaware became the first state to ratify the Constitution. By the summer of 1788, nine states had approved the document. The Constitution was now the supreme law of the land.

In time, all 13 states approved the Constitution. However, some states, like Virginia, insisted that a Bill of Rights be added to the original document. They wanted certain freedoms to be clearly protected. Therefore, in 1791, this Bill of Rights became the first ten **amendments** to the Constitution.

Government Fact

The Federalist Papers are still admired today. They clearly show how political ideas apply to everyday life.

Citizenship and You

LOOKING AT BOTH SIDES OF AN ISSUE

The national debate over the ratification of the Constitution was one of the most famous debates in U.S. history. Both sides presented very good arguments for their positions. Both sides felt they had the best interests of the country at heart.

Review what you have already read about the development of government in the United States from colonial times up through the Constitutional Convention. Write two or three paragraphs making the strongest case you can for the Federalist position. Then write two or three paragraphs making the strongest case you can for the anti-Federalist position.

After the Constitution was ratified, George Washington became the first President of the United States.

LANDMARK CHANGES IN THE LAW
The United States Gets a Constitution

The delegates to the Convention began their meetings on May 25, 1787. For the next three and a half months, through a hot Philadelphia summer, the debate went on. The Constitutional Convention was a meeting of the brightest, richest men in the country. Benjamin Franklin was there, along with George Washington, James Madison, and more than 50 others. They met in secret to write the laws that would form a new government. Luckily, James Madison took many notes about what happened each day. Today, we have a good record of what went on.

At times, angry words were traded back and forth. Some days there seemed to be no way to reach a compromise. Benjamin Franklin even asked the group to begin each day's meeting with a prayer.

Most of the men were well to do lawyers, teachers, or landowners. Most of the country was made up of poor farmers and working people. Because of this, it could be said that this meeting was not truly representative of "the people." However, working people could not afford to take three or four months off to do the work of government. The men at the Convention had worked for years in government. Eleven years earlier, some of them had signed the Declaration of Independence. Most of them had served in colonial assemblies or in their own state governments. They all believed strongly in the rights of the people and in limited government.

Thirty-nine representatives signed the Constitution on September 17, 1787. The final document contained ideas from the Magna Carta, English written law, and several state constitutions. In addition, it fulfilled the wishes of one delegate who spoke during the Convention. He said that the Constitution should be written not "for the moment, but for future generations of Americans."

You Decide

Was the average citizen of the United States fairly represented at the Constitutional Convention? Why or why not?

Summary

After the signing of the Declaration of Independence, most of the states drew up written constitutions.

The Articles of Confederation was the first written plan of government for the United States. The Articles proved to be a weak plan for a government.

In 1787, the Continental Congress asked the states to send representatives to Philadelphia to make changes in the Articles. The representatives wrote a whole new plan of government.

The new Constitution contained ideas from the Magna Carta, English written law, and several state constitutions.

Federalists thought the Constitution was a good mixture of federal power and state power. Anti-Federalists felt the Constitution went too far in taking power away from the states.

By the summer of 1788, the necessary nine states had ratified the Constitution. In 1791, the Bill of Rights, which protected certain rights, became the first ten amendments to the Constitution.

Constitutional Convention

export

confederation

federal government

slave

Vocabulary Review

Write a term from the list that matches each definition below.

1. This meeting was held in Philadelphia in 1787

2. An agreement between states

3. A person who could be bought or sold

4. Something made in one country and bought by another country

5. A form of government with two parts

Chapter Quiz

Complete numbers 1–5 by choosing the correct word or phrase. Then answer questions 6 and 7 in complete sentences.

1. One of the five main ideas of government the state constitutions were based on was (one-man rule/separation of powers).

2. Under the Articles of Confederation, the Congress had (great/limited) powers.

3. The delegates to the 1787 Philadelphia Convention (changed the Articles/wrote a new plan for government).

4. The Great Compromise at the Convention involved (slavery/representation in Congress).

5. Before the Constitution became law, it had to be (ratified/changed) by nine states.

6. **Critical Thinking** Why did the state constitutions written after the Declaration of Independence give power to the people?

7. **Critical Thinking** Why were the anti-Federalists against the Constitution?

Write About Government

Complete the following activities.

1. The Articles of Confederation set up a weak federal government. List three problems that this caused for the newly independent United States.

2. You are a newspaper reporter in 1787. Write a short newspaper story about the new Constitution.

Chapter 4

A Close Look at the Constitution

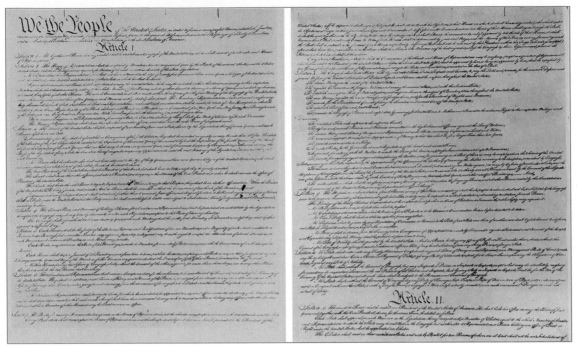

The first section of the U.S. Constitution is shown in the photograph above.

Learning Objectives

- Identify the basic principles behind the Constitution.
- Explain how the Constitution sets up the federal government in seven articles.
- Explain the meaning and importance of the Bill of Rights.

Words to Know

legislative branch	the part of government that makes the laws
executive branch	the part of government that carries out the laws
judicial branch	the part of government that rules on what the laws mean
trial	a case heard at court before a judge or jury
senator	a member of the Senate
unconstitutional	a law or government act that goes against the Constitution

The Basic Principles Behind the Constitution

On July 4, 1788, the people of Philadelphia turned out for a parade. They cheered loudly for a model ship named *Constitution*. The ship stood for the new government of the United States. The people hoped the new government would be lasting. They wanted to see the country grow strong over the coming years.

In 1987, people all over the world celebrated the 200th anniversary of the writing of the Constitution. The government that had been set up more than 200 years ago in Philadelphia had indeed lasted. It lasted through many changes and many tough times. The United States started as a small country with a few million people, most of whom were farmers. Today, it is a country with hundreds of thousands of different businesses and a population of more than 270 million. Remarkably, in more than 220 years, the Constitution has been changed only 27 times.

The Constitution written in 1787 sets up a plan for government in seven articles. That plan is based on the following principles.

1. **Rule by the people** In a democracy, the people hold the power to make all the laws.

2. **Limited powers** Government must not be too strong; freedoms must be protected.

3. **Separation of powers** Power in government is divided among three branches: the **legislative branch**, the **executive branch**, and the **judicial branch**.

4. **Checks and balances** Each branch of government has some powers over the other branches.

5. **Judicial review** The state courts must throw out any state laws that go against the U.S. Constitution.

6. **Federal government** The United States government has some powers. The state governments have their own powers.

Remember
You have already read about most of these principles. You can turn back to Chapter 3 for a review.

Freedom of religion is guaranteed to all Americans by the First Amendment of the Constitution.

Outline of the U.S. Constitution

Article	What the Article Does
Preamble	**opening words:** tells why the Constitution was written
Article I	**legislative branch:** sets up a way to make laws (Congress)
Article II	**executive branch:** sets up a way to carry out the laws (the President and Vice President)
Article III	**judicial branch:** sets up a way to judge the laws (the Supreme Court and the lower federal courts)
Article IV	**the states:** says that states must honor each others' laws; sets rules for admitting new states; guarantees republican government in states
Article V	**amendments:** sets up a way to change the Constitution
Article VI	**supreme law:** states that the Constitution is the highest law of the land
Article VII	**ratification:** sets up how the states must vote for the Constitution to become law

Amendments to the U.S. Constitution

Amendment	Year Adopted	What the Amendment Does
First	1791	Protects freedom of religion, speech, press, and assembly
Second	1791	Protects the right to bear arms; states may have an emergency army
Third	1791	Protects people from having to house soldiers during peacetime
Fourth	1791	Protects people and their property from government searches without good reason
Fifth	1791	Sets up grand jury; protects citizens against having to face **trial** more than once; guarantees due process
Sixth	1791	Guarantees fair and quick trial for accused persons
Seventh	1791	Guarantees a jury trial for court cases
Eighth	1791	Guarantees reasonable treatment and punishment for accused persons
Ninth	1791	Reserves for the people all rights not listed in the Constitution
Tenth	1791	Saves all other powers for the states and people

The Bill of Rights (Amendments 1–10)

Amendments to the U.S. Constitution

Amendment	Year Adopted	What the Amendment Does
Eleventh	1798	Protects states from federal lawsuits
Twelfth	1804	Requires a separate vote for President and a separate vote for Vice President in elections
Thirteenth	1865	Ends slavery in the United States
Fourteenth	1868	Grants citizenship to African Americans; protects people's rights from unfair treatment by state governments
Fifteenth	1870	Grants African Americans the right to vote
Sixteenth	1913	Sets up a federal income tax
Seventeenth	1913	Allows people of each state to directly elect their own senators to Congress
Eighteenth	1919	Outlaws manufacture, sale, and transportation of alcoholic beverages
Nineteenth	1920	Grants women the right to vote
Twentieth	1933	Sets dates for the beginning of Congress's meetings and President's term of office

Amendments to the U.S. Constitution

Amendment	Year Adopted	What the Amendment Does
Twenty-First	1933	Repeals, or ends, the Eighteenth Amendment
Twenty-Second	1951	Allows President to have only two elected terms
Twenty-Third	1961	Grants citizens of Washington, D.C. the right to vote for President
Twenty-Fourth	1964	Ends taxes on voting in national elections (poll tax)
Twenty-Fifth	1967	Sets guidelines for filling the offices of President and Vice President should they become vacant
Twenty-Sixth	1971	Grants 18-year-olds the right to vote
Twenty-Seventh	1992	Stops Congress from increasing the salary of its current members

✔ **Check Your Understanding**

1. List the basic principles behind the U.S. Constitution.

2. Write your own brief description of the First, Fourth, and Fifth amendments to the Constitution.

A Plan for Government in Seven Articles

Remember
You can read the entire Constitution on pages 319–350 of this book.

The Preamble The Constitution opens with a few words that tell you its purpose. These words are called the Preamble. It states that the Constitution is to set up ways to keep the country safe, peaceful, and fair in its laws.

Articles I–III: Separation of Powers The first three articles separate the powers of government into three branches. Each branch is given some powers over the other two branches.

Article I: The Legislative Branch This article creates a Congress with the power to make laws. It lists its powers and duties. Congress is set up in two houses. One is the Senate. The other is the House of Representatives.

Article II: The Executive Branch This article describes the duties of the President. It gives the President the power to carry out laws and to represent our country in dealings with other countries. The President is also the head of all the country's armed forces. The President can ask for laws to be passed that will help the country. The President must also report to Congress on the well-being of the country.

Article III: The Judicial Branch This article creates the Supreme Court, the highest court in the land. This article gives the Court the power to decide final appeals of all cases. It decides whether laws follow the Constitution. The article also gives Congress the power to set up lower federal courts.

Article IV: State Governments All states have to honor the laws of the other states. If you are married in California, then you are still married when you visit Florida.

In addition, if citizens have rights and privileges in one state, these rights are guaranteed in the others, too. Suppose you live in a state where you can drive at age 16. What happens when you drive into a state where you have to be 18 to drive? Although you are underage, you can still drive in the state you are visiting.

Article IV also guarantees that each state will have a government with three branches. Therefore, in every state, you find a legislative, an executive, and a judicial branch.

Article V: Making Changes This article describes the methods for making changes, or amendments, to the Constitution. The idea of allowing the Constitution to be changed goes along with the idea of government by the people. The people made the Constitution, so the people can change it.

However, the writers of the Constitution did not make it easy to amend it. Ideas for amendments must be passed by two-thirds of the Congress. In other words, 67 out of 100 senators must vote for any change. In addition, 290 out of 435 representatives must vote for it. After that, three-fourths of the states, either in their legislatures or in special conventions, must also pass the amendment. That means that 38 states must ratify the amendment.

There is another method for amending the Constitution. Two-thirds of the states (34 states) can ask Congress to call a national convention to propose an amendment. Then the amendment must be ratified by three-fourths of the states. This can be done either in their legislatures or in special conventions.

History Fact

Since the Constitution was signed, more than 6,000 ideas for amendments have been written. Only 27 have been passed into law.

Article VI: The Constitution Is Supreme Law The Sixth Article makes the Constitution the highest law of the land. All representatives and leaders in government must swear to obey and uphold the Constitution.

All state and federal laws in the land must uphold the Constitution. If a state or federal law seems to go against the Constitution, it can be challenged before the Supreme Court. If the court finds that the law is **unconstitutional**, the law is struck down. Here, for example, are some laws that would be unconstitutional.

- A state raises its voting age to 21.

- A state sets up a dictatorship.

- Congress passes a law to end the presidency.

Article VII: Ratification The Constitution had to be ratified, or passed, by the states in order for it to become law. Each state sent representatives to its own constitutional convention. Nine of the thirteen states had to ratify the Constitution before it would take effect.

History Fact

Almost two years went by before the necessary nine states ratified the Constitution. Only after the Bill of Rights was added did all 13 states ratify it.

✓ **Check Your Understanding**

1. Write one or two sentences describing the purpose of the Constitution.

2. Describe the powers the Constitution gives to the judicial branch of government.

3. What does the Constitution say about state governments?

Government Skills

STUDYING IMPORTANT DOCUMENTS

To understand the U.S. system of government, you must first understand the documents that established it. The two most important documents in our history are the Declaration of Independence and the Constitution.

Both of these documents are reprinted in Appendix A and Appendix B in the back of this book. They are printed in their original words. Parts of them may be difficult to understand. In studying these important documents, look up any unfamiliar words in a dictionary.

A. The Declaration of Independence is written in three sections. Read each section carefully. Then answer these questions.

1. In Section One, what three rights should all people enjoy?

2. In Section One, what can the people do if their government destroys or ignores these rights?

3. What are four charges made against the king in Section Two?

4. What are three things listed in Section Three that the new "free and independent" states have the power to do?

B. Study the first three articles of the Constitution. Then answer these questions.

1. What section of Article I describes the powers of Congress? List five of these powers.

2. What section of Article II describes the powers of the President? List three powers of the President.

3. What section of Article III tells who has the power to create the courts below the Supreme Court? Who has this power?

LANDMARK CHANGES IN THE LAW
The Bill of Rights

By the summer of 1788, nine states had ratified the Constitution, and there was strong support for passage in the remaining states. Still, many people felt the Constitution needed to be strengthened. They thought it did not provide enough protection for the rights of individual citizens.

The first session of Congress was held in March 1789. The new lawmakers soon took up the matter of making changes to the Constitution. James Madison, a member of the House of Representatives, suggested nine amendments. These additions spelled out many basic rights for the people. During the next few months, other congressmen made suggestions as well. Finally, in the fall of 1789, 12 amendments were proposed to the states to be ratified.

Thomas Jefferson must have been particularly pleased. As the author of the Declaration of Independence, he was a strong believer in individual freedoms. He had supported passage of the Constitution on one condition—Congress would have to add a listing of basic rights immediately after it began its first session.

In December 1791, the states ratified 10 of the 12 amendments. These amendments as a group became known as the Bill of Rights. Together, they established the great freedoms we cherish: freedom of the press, speech, and religion; freedom of security of the person; and fair and equal protection under the law. These first "changes" to the Constitution created an even stronger foundation for government. In time, they were used to guarantee to all Americans the basic rights fought for and won in the War for Independence.

You Decide

Do you think it was necessary for the states to pass a Bill of Rights spelling out protection of certain freedoms? Why or why not?

Summary

These are the basic principles behind the U.S. Constitution: (1) rule by the people, (2) limited powers, (3) separation of powers, (4) checks and balances, (5) judicial review, and (6) federal government.
The legislative branch (Congress) makes the laws. The executive branch (the President) carries out the laws. The judicial branch (the Supreme Court) judges the laws.
Article IV says that all states must honor the laws of other states.
Article V describes the methods for making changes (amendments) to the Constitution.
Article VI makes the Constitution the supreme law of the land. All states must uphold the Constitution.
The first ten amendments to the Constitution are called the Bill of Rights. These amendments protect many personal freedoms and rights.

trial

legislative branch

executive branch

judicial branch

senator

unconstitutional

Vocabulary Review

Complete each sentence with a term from the list.

1. Something is _____ if it violates the Constitution.

2. The _____ interprets what is legal.

3. Laws are made by the _____.

4. A judge can determine the outcome of a _____.

5. The _____ makes sure that the laws are followed.

6. A member of the Senate is called a _____.

Chapter Quiz

Write your answers in complete sentences.

1. What part of the Constitution tells its purpose?

2. What principle of government do the first three articles of the Constitution establish?

3. Which member of the House of Representatives first proposed amendments to protect freedoms and rights?

4. How many amendments have been added to the Constitution up to the present day?

5. Which amendment ended, or repealed, an earlier amendment?

6. **Critical Thinking** Explain the separation of powers. Why do you think the writers of the Constitution created that system?

7. **Critical Thinking** How were the rights of African Americans guaranteed in the Constitution?

Write About Government

Complete the following activities.

1. The Constitution says that all states must honor the laws of other states. Give a few examples of the kinds of laws the states must honor.

2. What laws would the Supreme Court say are unconstitutional? Give examples.

Unit 1 **Review**

Comprehension Check
Complete the sentences by choosing the correct word or phrase.

1. The ancient Greeks were the first people to practice (representative government/direct democracy).

2. The ancient Romans had (two leaders with sole government power/laws written into codes).

3. The Magna Carta promised (certain rights to the upper classes/certain rights to all English people).

4. The Pilgrims signed the Mayflower Compact in order to (declare their independence from England/set up a government for themselves in North America).

5. The Articles of Confederation (set up the first government of the United States/were ratified by Britain's Parliament).

6. At the Constitutional Convention, the Great Compromise (ended slavery after 20 years/created two houses of Congress).

7. The U.S. Constitution (set up a government with checks and balances/created an independent United States).

8. The Bill of Rights (set up three branches of government/protects many personal freedoms).

Writing an Essay
Answer one of the following essay topics.

1. Discuss different forms of democracy that have existed in various countries over time.

2. Explain the differences and similarities between the monarchy in England and the newly formed American democracy.

3. Discuss the major events that led to the ratification of the United States Constitution.

Government in Your Life
Which amendment to the Constitution has most affected your life? Explain your answer.

Unit ▶2 The Federal Government

Chapter 5

Congress, the Legislative Branch

The House of Representatives is sworn in before each new session of Congress.

Learning Objectives

- Name and describe the two houses of Congress.
- Explain the differences between the House of Representatives and the Senate.
- Explain the duties and responsibilities of committees of Congress.
- List and describe the powers of Congress.

Words to Know

session	the meetings of Congress that begin in January each year
committee	a group of representatives and senators in Congress; it meets to study bills, learn about problems in the country, and find ways to solve them
majority	more than half
bill	an idea for new laws that is written and voted on
standing committee	House and Senate study group that studies the same problems from year to year
constituents	the people who elect a person to public office

The People's Branch of Government

Have you ever questioned why a letter took so long to be delivered? Have you thought that too much money was taken out of your paycheck to pay taxes? If so, you may have said, "There ought to be a law!"

Only one branch of the federal government can decide if "there ought to be a law." It is the Congress of the United States. Congress is often called the "people's branch" of government. All members of Congress are elected by the people. Most other members of the federal government are picked by the elected leaders. Members of Congress are the federal leaders who are closest to us all.

Who are the people in Congress? They come from many different backgrounds. They are all elected by people in their home states. They have the duty of serving the best interests of all the people they represent.

At the same time, they must serve the best interests of the states they represent. However, their main job is to make our country's laws.

Meetings of Congress

Each year in January, Congress begins a new **session**. The session meets day-to-day during most of the year. The meetings take place in the huge, white Capitol building. It sits on top of Capitol Hill in the center of Washington, D.C. The Capitol has two large meeting rooms where each house of Congress meets. It has smaller meeting rooms where **committees** meet.

The House of Representatives

The House of Representatives is the larger house of Congress. It has 435 members. Each member has one vote. Some states have large populations. Those states have the most seats in the House. California has more than 29 million people. It sends 52 representatives to the House. Rhode Island has about one million people. It elects only two representatives.

The House of Representatives is often called the lower house of Congress. Representatives serve short terms of only two years. Each member represents only a part of a state, called a district. Representatives usually closely follow the wishes of the voters. Otherwise, they might not be reelected after two years.

Speaker of the House

At the beginning of each two-year term of Congress, the representatives elect a leader. The leader is called the Speaker of the House. The Speaker must be elected by a majority of House members.

The leader of the political party with the most members—the **majority** party—is normally elected

Speaker. The Speaker is a very powerful person who runs the sessions of the House and keeps order. No member can speak unless "recognized" by the Speaker. The Speaker also applies all the rules of the House, sends **bills** to committees, and can also appoint members to committees. Once elected, a Speaker may hold the office through many sessions of Congress, as long as his or her party is in power.

Sam Rayburn was Speaker of the House longer than any other Speaker in history.

The Senate

The Senate is much smaller than the House of Representatives. The Senate has only 100 members. Each of the 50 states elects two senators.

The Senate is known as the upper house of Congress. A senator represents all the people of a state. Senators serve for six years, three times longer than representatives to the House. Senators have to face elections only once every six years. They are less tied to what their state's voters want. They have more freedom to decide what will be good for the whole country in coming years.

President of the Senate

The Senate's leader is called the "president of the Senate." The Constitution gives this job to the Vice President. The Vice President has much less power than the Speaker does in the House. The Vice President:

- is not a senator.

- cannot speak for or against a bill.

- can vote only to break a tie.

- does not have to vote.

Today, the Vice President has many other jobs besides being President of the Senate. Often, the Vice President is away on other business. Then the Senate is led by a president pro tempore. *Pro tempore* means "for the time being." The president pro tempore is elected by the Senate itself. Usually, the president pro tempore is a leading member of the majority party.

Committees of Congress

The House and Senate leaders help Congress get through a great load of work. Yet much of the day-to-day work in both houses is done by committees. These groups study the different problems facing the country. They ask questions such as these.

- What can the government do to help homeless people?

- How can the government pay off the money it owes?

- How can young people be kept safe from street drugs?

Every member of Congress serves on at least one committee. The committees meet to learn about a problem. They study bills that could help solve the problems.

The Standing Committees

The most important committees in Congress are the **standing committees**. Each standing committee has a special interest. One Senate committee may study bills having to do only with the armed services. One House committee may study bills about the post office. Committees gather as many facts as possible before deciding on a bill. They listen to people speak for and against it. Then committee members talk over the bill among themselves.

The House has 19 standing committees. The Senate has 21. The members of a standing committee may change from one election to the next. However, the kinds of problems each committee studies stay the same.

The representatives and senators on standing committees have much power. They decide which bills will have a chance to become laws. If they decide "no" on a bill, that bill will almost certainly be voted down by the full membership. Many times a "no" vote means the bill will not even reach the full House or Senate for a vote.

The Powers of Congress

Article I, Section 8 of the Constitution lists the powers of Congress. Some of these powers are described below.

- Congress can raise and collect taxes to pay for the work of the federal government. This includes paying employees and paying for federal programs that can help the people of the country. Congress can print money and set its value. It can also borrow money for the country.

- Congress can make rules for trade and business between the United States and other countries. It can also make rules for trade and business between the states.

- Congress can establish and make rules for the postal system (post offices). Congress also runs the national highway system, national parks, and all federal buildings.

- Congress protects the nation against enemies. It can declare war, and it can raise and support armies and navies.

- Congress can establish all federal courts below the Supreme Court and set their rules.

Limits on Congress

The Constitution also puts limits on what Congress can do. These limits fall into two areas. There are things that members of Congress cannot do because the Constitution does not grant the power to do them. In addition, there are things Congress cannot do because the Constitution forbids them.

Here are some things Congress has not been granted the power to do. Congress cannot pass laws to:
- create a national school system.

- set rules for marriage and divorce.

- set a minimum age for drivers' licenses.

- set rules for units of local governments.

Here are some things Congress has been forbidden from doing by the Constitution. Congress cannot:
- order that people be held in prison without their rights except when public safety is threatened.

- take money from the federal government without first passing a law to do so.

- tax any goods exported from states.

- grant titles of nobility—like king, queen, or prince—to any person.

Citizenship and You

WRITING LAWMAKERS

Most Senators and representatives look forward to hearing from their **constituents**. Members of Congress need to know the voters' ideas on what to do about the country's problems. Receiving advice from "back home" helps the members do their jobs better.

The lawmakers try to answer all the mail they receive. The first step is to find out who your representative and senators are. You can write them to find out what bills and problems are being studied now in Congress. Follow the steps below to contact your representative and senators.

1. Look in your phone book under "U.S. Government" for the local addresses of your representative and senators. You can find their Washington, D.C., addresses on the Internet.

2. Write one letter to your representative. Write two others, one to each of your state's two senators. You can reach them through the e-mail address, or use the following addresses.

   To: Representative _____
   House Office Building
   Washington, D.C. 20515

   To: Senator _____
   Senate Office Building
   Washington, D.C. 20510

3. In your letters, ask for a list of bills that are before the House or Senate. Ask each lawmaker which committee(s) he or she is a member of. Ask which bills each lawmaker has written or helped to write. Then choose one issue or problem in your town or state that interests you. Ask your representative (town) or senators (state) what can be done about it.

The Elastic Clause

Congress has other powers that are not specifically named in the Constitution. The last part of Article I, Section 8 says that Congress can make all laws "necessary and proper" to carry out its duties. This part of the Constitution has come to be called the "elastic clause." Congress has used the clause to pass laws that are not listed in the Constitution.

✓ Check Your Understanding

1. List three powers the Constitution gives to Congress.

2. In what ways does the Constitution put a limit on the powers of Congress?

One of the Senate's roles is to confirm or reject presidential appointees. Shown here is Supreme Court nominee Judge Ruth Bader Ginsburg just before the start of her confirmation hearing. Ginsburg's nomination for the Supreme Court was confirmed.

LANDMARK CHANGES IN THE LAW
McCulloch v. Maryland

In the early days of the United States, Congress set up a federal bank. The bank was created to help the federal government carry out its powers to tax, borrow, and print money. Many people in the states were against the idea of a federal bank. They felt it gave too much power to the national government.

Some states passed laws to force the federal bank in their state to fail. In 1818, Maryland passed such a law. It was a tax on all money issued by the federal bank in the state. The bank's cashier, James McCulloch, purposely issued money without paying the tax. The state took him to court. The highest court in Maryland ruled against McCulloch and the bank.

The federal government, on behalf of McCulloch, appealed to the U.S. Supreme Court. Maryland argued that the bank went against the Constitution. The state said Congress was not given the power to set up a bank. The federal government argued that Article I, Section 8 of the Constitution allowed Congress to carry out its named powers. The government said the bank did just that. It helped carry out trade between the states. In addition, it helped to raise and borrow money. The government also argued that no state could tax an agency of the federal government.

In 1819, the Supreme Court ruled unanimously in favor of the federal government. The Court said it was necessary and proper for Congress to use the bank to carry out its powers. The Court also said that no state could ever tax the United States or any of its agencies.

The case of *McCulloch* v. *Maryland* tested the powers of the states against the powers of the federal government. The Supreme Court's ruling strengthened the powers of Congress under the elastic clause.

You Decide

Do you think the Supreme Court was right in stretching the elastic clause the way it did? Why or why not?

Summary

Congress is the lawmaking branch of government. It has two houses: the House of Representatives and the Senate.

The House of Representatives, the lower house of Congress, has 435 members. The members serve two-year terms. Representation is based on the population of a state. The leader of the House of Representatives is the Speaker of the House.

The Senate, the upper house of Congress, has 100 members. Each state elects two senators. Members serve six-year terms. The Constitution gives the Vice President the job of leader of the Senate. When the Vice President is away, the Senate is led by a president pro tempore.

Both the House and Senate use standing committees to study problems and ideas for laws.

Congress has many powers. The Constitution also puts limits on the powers of Congress. In the case of *McCulloch* v. *Maryland*, the Supreme Court ruled that Congress had certain powers not spelled out in the Constitution.

Vocabulary Review

Write *true* or *false*. If the statement is false, change the underlined term to make it true.

1. The <u>majority</u> is more than half.

2. <u>Constituents</u> elect members of Congress.

3. A <u>committee</u> of Congress begins in January.

4. All <u>standing</u> <u>committees</u> deal with the same issue every year.

5. Members of Congress vote on ideas for new laws, or <u>sessions</u>.

Chapter Quiz

Complete numbers 1–6 by filling in the correct word or phrase. Then answer questions 7 and 8 in complete sentences.

1. Congressional sessions begin each year in _____.

2. The Speaker of the House is normally the leader of the _____.

3. Members of the Senate represent _____ of a state.

4. As the president of the Senate, the Vice President can only vote _____.

5. Standing committees of Congress decide which bills _____.

6. The Constitution gives powers to Congress in Article _____, Section _____.

7. Critical Thinking What are some of the differences between standing committees and other committees in Congress?

8. Critical Thinking Why do you think the Constitution gives Congress additional powers in the "elastic clause"?

Write About Government

Complete the following activity.

Choose one of the following standing committees of Congress. Give a brief description of the committees' duties and responsibilities. The following Web site is a good source of information: www.loc.gov/global/legislative/congress.html.

House Ways and Means Committee
House Appropriations Committee
House Agriculture Committee

Senate Judiciary Committee
Senate Armed Services Committee
Senate Foreign Relations Committee

Chapter 6

How Federal Laws Are Made

This is the Capitol Building in Washington, D.C.

Learning Objectives

- Explain where the ideas for laws may come from.
- Name the six steps it takes for a bill to become a law.
- Give two reasons why a bill might fail to become a law.

Words to Know

testify	to make statements in hearings or in court to establish some truth or fact
subcommittee	a branch of a standing committee that has a special area of study
conference committee	a House-Senate committee that works out the differences in bills passed by the two houses of Congress
presiding officer	the leader of a government body who runs or directs that body
legislation	laws that are made or proposed
floor leader	the leader of each of the two political parties in Congress who directs the debate on proposed bills
whip	the assistant to each of the floor leaders of Congress

Where Laws Come From

Every two years, thousands of bills are introduced in Congress. Fewer than 100 of these bills become laws. Turning a bill into a law is a long and often hard job. Making laws takes many steps.

Every law starts with an idea. This idea may come from one of many places. Farm workers may wish to outlaw the spraying of a poison on crops. The President's office may wish to pay for ads about the dangers of drug use. A senator from Arizona may want to bring water to dry land. These ideas all come from different places. However, each must travel the same path before it can become law.

How a Bill Becomes a Law

Every law begins as a bill in Congress. New tax bills must start in the House of Representatives. All other bills may start in either the House or the Senate. Bills must then go through at least six important steps to become laws. (See the chart on page 77.)

Step 1. Introducing the Bill Suppose a representative named Joan Atkins has an idea for a new law. Many businesses in her home state of Massachusetts have a problem. They are not making enough money to pay their workers. Many people in Massachusetts have lost their jobs.

Atkins thinks businesses should pay workers with some of the money they pay in taxes. She wants to cut federal taxes for businesses. Atkins writes her ideas for a new law in a bill. Then she brings her bill to the large meeting room of the House. She drops it into a wooden box called the "hopper."

The Clerk of the House then gives the bill a number and a short title. The title and a very brief description of Atkins's bill are printed in the *Congressional Record*. This action is called the first reading of the bill. The bill is then printed so that all members may have copies to read. Next, the Speaker of the House sends Atkins's bill to the proper standing committee.

Step 2. The Committee Stage Atkins's bill is sent to the House Ways and Means Committee. This is the House committee that handles all tax bills.

Members of the committee study the bill carefully. They listen to Atkins explain how the future law will work. They listen to other representatives speak for or against the bill. The committee asks many questions: Will the bill really help keep people working? Who could be harmed by the bill? Is there a better way to

The House Ways and Means Committee works on changing the tax laws. The federal government has placed a tax on gasoline.

help businesses and workers? Sometimes, the committee will hold public hearings. Experts in the field, government officials, and other interested persons may be invited to **testify**.

A Committee Within a Committee

A standing committee often turns over its work on a proposed bill to one of its **subcommittees**. A subcommittee has a special area of interest. Its members, who also serve on the larger standing committee, are usually experts in this one area. They can devote their time to studying this area closely. Then they make recommendations to the full committee. There are about 140 subcommittees in the House and more than 100 in the Senate.

After several meetings, the committee votes. Some representatives vote for the bill, some against it. The bill passes. It now goes before the whole House of Representatives.

Step 3. The Debate As the general debate begins, the bill receives its second reading, section by section. Each representative in the House may debate the bill on the floor. Representatives are allowed up to one hour to speak. Atkins speaks first. She asks the House to pass the bill.

A representative from Kansas speaks next. He explains that the bill will not help his state. Kansas has mostly farms and fewer businesses. If businesses get a tax break, he says, farmers should, too.

Then a representative from New York speaks against the bill. She does not want businesses to get a tax cut. If they do, the federal government will have less money for helping poor people.

Finally, a representative from Texas speaks. He wants the bill to pass. Lower taxes will help businesses grow. As they grow, they will put more people to work. As more people work, other workers will be needed, such as builders or truckers.

The debate goes on for hours. When the debate ends, the bill is printed in its final form. Then it is given a third reading. Finally, the House votes—235 representatives are for the bill; 200 are against it. Atkins's bill has passed in the House.

Step 4. On to the Senate Atkins's bill now goes to the Senate Finance Committee. This committee, like the House Ways and Means Committee, studies all tax bills. After more hearings, the committee votes on the bill. The bill passes and goes before the full Senate.

Debating begins again. A senator from Iowa adds an amendment to the bill. This change reduces the tax cut for businesses. The amendment creates added support for the bill. On the next Senate vote, the bill passes.

Step 5. Conference Committee Both houses of Congress have passed Representative Atkins's tax bill. However, since the Senate amended the bill, the two houses have passed different bills. What happens now? A special **conference committee** must make both bills agree.

Members of both houses make up this special committee. It meets in secret. The committee can only consider the points on which the two bills disagree. After much work, members finally agree on the bill.

Both houses of Congress must pass the new compromise bill. No amendments can be added to it now. The committee's changes are agreeable to a majority in both houses. The bill passes easily. It is almost a law.

Senator Ben Nighthorse Campbell from Colorado, who serves as a member of several conference committees, meets with the press at a national park.

FOCUS ON GOVERNMENT
Congressional Floor Leaders

In the last chapter, you learned about the leaders of the House and the Senate. The Speaker of the House and the Vice President of the United States are the **presiding officers** of those two bodies. However, when **legislation** is being considered, other leaders play more important roles. The **floor leaders** of the two political parties—Democrat and Republican—have a lot of control during the lawmaking steps.

Both the House of Representatives and the Senate have majority and minority leaders. These leaders are elected by their parties at the beginning of the session of Congress. The majority leader in both houses is the leader of the party with the most members in that body. The minority leaders are the leaders of the smaller party.

The floor leaders plan the best course of action to see that the wishes of their party are carried out. They try to steer the floor action to their party's benefit.

The majority leader in both houses is the more important position. That is simply because the leader's party has the most votes. However, the majority and minority leaders do work together. They decide how and when a bill will be considered. They plan how the debate will proceed. In addition, they make sure each side gets a fair hearing of its position.

The two party leaders have assistants—majority and minority **whips**. The whips' main job is to keep in close contact with the party members. Then the whips can inform the leaders how many votes will be "for" or "against" any particular bill.

As a congressional floor leader, Senate Majority Leader Trent Lott, of Mississippi, discusses issues with senior Republican committee members.

Using a Filibuster

Each member of the House of Representatives can speak only for one hour on a bill. However, senators can speak for as long as they like. Some senators try to kill a bill by speaking so long that the Senate must go on to other business. This delaying method is called a *filibuster*.

A senator once spoke on the Senate floor for 15 hours straight. He read from a telephone book and a mail-order catalog, and he gave his fellow senators homemade food recipes.

The Senate can end a filibuster by voting for the *cloture* rule. If three-fifths of the Senate (60 senators) votes for cloture, the filibuster is cut off. Each member is then allowed no more than one hour to speak. Then a final vote must be taken.

Step 6. The President's Desk Atkins's bill now goes to the President of the United States. Every bill Congress passes goes to the President. One of four things can happen. The President can:

1. Sign the bill so it becomes a law.

2. Veto, or stop, the bill. If the President vetoes the bill, it returns to Congress. If two-thirds of both houses vote for it, the bill still becomes a law. This is called overriding a veto.

3. Leave the bill unsigned for ten days while Congress is in session. Then it automatically becomes law. The President does not have to sign it.

4. Leave the bill unsigned for ten days after Congress has ended its session. Then the bill dies.

What will the President do with Representative Atkins's bill? Since both houses of Congress liked the bill very much, the President thinks the bill is probably good for most of the country. He then signs it.

Representative Atkins calls home to share the good news. Businesses will save money on taxes next year. Her bill is now a law!

Remember
In the system of checks and balances, the power of Congress to override a veto is a check on the Executive branch.

Government Skills

READING A FLOW CHART

A flow chart shows the steps for doing something. The chart on page 77 shows the steps in making a law. Arrows flow from one step to the next. Answer these questions to help you understand the chart.

- What are the first and last steps in lawmaking?

- Name the different committees the bill goes to.

- What happens just before the President gets the bill?

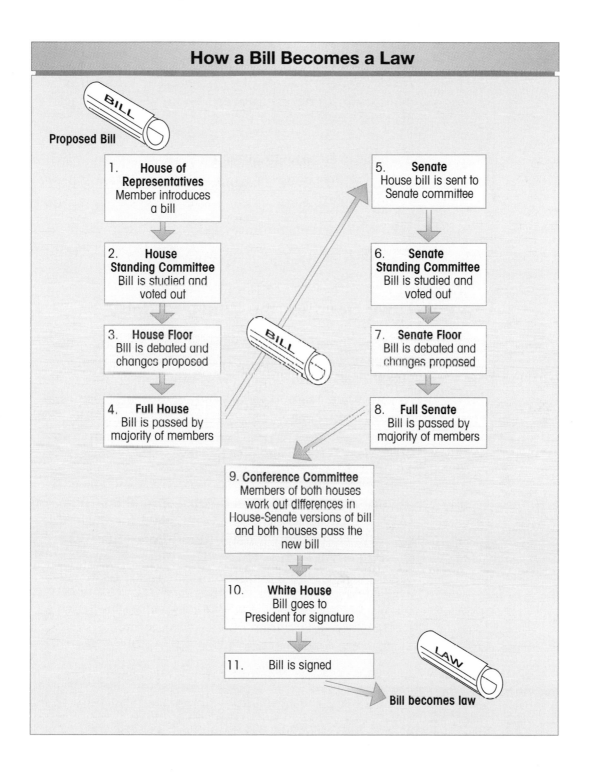

How a Bill Becomes a Law

Proposed Bill

1. **House of Representatives**
Member introduces a bill

2. **House Standing Committee**
Bill is studied and voted out

3. **House Floor**
Bill is debated and changes proposed

4. **Full House**
Bill is passed by majority of members

5. **Senate**
House bill is sent to Senate committee

6. **Senate Standing Committee**
Bill is studied and voted out

7. **Senate Floor**
Bill is debated and changes proposed

8. **Full Senate**
Bill is passed by majority of members

9. **Conference Committee**
Members of both houses work out differences in House-Senate versions of bill and both houses pass the new bill

10. **White House**
Bill goes to President for signature

11. Bill is signed

Bill becomes law

Two important checks and balances are built into the steps for making laws. The President's veto is a check over the powers of Congress. The two-thirds majority in Congress to override the veto is a check over the powers of the President.

✓ Check Your Understanding

1. In which house of Congress must all tax bills start?

2. What do subcommittees do?

3. What do conference committees do?

Laws Good for the Whole Country

Many months of hard work go into making a law. However, most bills never become laws. Many are killed in committee. Some pass one house, only to die in the other. Members of Congress protect the special interests of the people they represent. That is why getting a majority of representatives and senators to agree on a bill can be difficult.

Suppose bills were easy to pass. Then each special interest group would have its own special laws. However, these laws might not be good for the whole country. That is why a majority of representatives must agree on each new law. This majority must represent the whole country, not just part of it.

GOVERNMENT ISSUES
Lobbyists and Special Interest Groups

A key feature of American government is representation of the people by elected officials or representatives. Part of the job of all representatives is to vote for laws that are best for the people who live in the district that elected them. For example, the representative of a farming district would probably be in favor of laws that are good for farmers.

Special interest groups are people, companies, or industries that feel strongly about a particular issue. These groups often hire lobbyists to help them get support for their interests. Lobbyists are people who represent the interests of a group. They work to persuade elected representatives to vote for a group's position on an issue. Lobbyists make presentations that give representatives detailed facts about issues. In this way, lobbyists help special interest groups try to persuade lawmakers to vote for their position.

Many citizens feel that lobbying is unfair. For example, large corporations or entire industries often spend millions of dollars lobbying for laws that help business. Some people feel that spending large amounts of money to gain the votes of lawmakers gives lobbies an unfair advantage over the interests of individual voters.

Currently, lobbying is permitted. However, it is controlled by rules and regulations. Lobbyists are not allowed to gain votes by making large contributions or giving special favors to elected representatives. The government and private groups of citizens watch lobbies and elected officials to make sure that the laws of lobbying are obeyed.

You Decide

Do you think lobbying is fair or unfair? Give reasons for your answer.

Summary

All federal laws begin in Congress as bills. Bills are studied in standing committees. Sometimes, they are turned over to subcommittees for closer study. All bills come to the floor of both houses of Congress for a full debate. Sometimes, amendments are added to bills during the floor debate.

Both houses must pass the same bill for it to become a law. If the House and the Senate pass bills that are different in some way, the two bills are sent to a conference committee.

Conference committees work out the differences in bills passed by the House and Senate.

When both houses pass the same bill, it goes to the President to be signed into law. If the President vetoes it, the bill is dead, unless Congress overrides the veto. It takes a two-thirds majority vote in both houses to override a veto.

legislation

whip

conference committee

subcommittee

testify

Vocabulary Review

Write the term from the list that matches the definition below.

1. To make a truthful statement

2. An assistant to each leader of Congress

3. Laws that are introduced to Congress

4. A group smaller than a standing committee

5. A combined House and Senate committee that works out the differences in bills

Chapter Quiz

Write your answers in complete sentences.

1. What kind of bills must always start in the House of Representatives?

2. What is a filibuster?

3. What is the job of a conference committee?

4. What *four* things can happen when a bill reaches the President's desk?

5. What are the *two* checks and balances built into the steps of lawmaking?

6. Critical Thinking Why do bills go to special committees?

7. Critical Thinking Why are the majority and minority whips important?

Write About Government

Complete the following activity.

Find a recent newspaper article that talks about a bill which was recently passed. Were your congressional representatives for or against the bill? You can check the Internet to see how they voted (www.vis.org). Make a list of reasons why you think they voted the way they did.

The White House is in Washington, D.C.

Learning Objectives

- Identify the six major ways the President leads the country.
- Explain the role and duties of the Vice President.
- Explain the role and duties of the special councils.
- Explain the role and duties of the Cabinet.

Words to Know

term	the length of time a person holds a government office
budget	a plan for spending money
ceremonial	done in a formal way for a special or important occasion
diplomat	a government official who works with governments of other countries
foreign policy	the course of action a country takes in relation to another country
treaty	an agreement between nations
ambassador	a representative of a government sent to a foreign country
Cabinet	the heads of the executive departments of the federal government
resign	to give up a position
council	a group of people who meet regularly to advise the President
environment	the air, water, and land that surround us

The President of the United States

The President is heard on radio and seen on television almost every day. You can read about him on the front page of almost every newspaper in the country. The President of the United States is known to millions of people around the world. The President makes news in many different ways.

Today, the President may be in Texas to ask people to vote for a woman running for office there. Tomorrow, he may meet with leaders from another country to talk about world trade. He might sign a new law to protect forests and wildlife, or throw out the first ball at the beginning of the baseball season.

History Fact

The United States has not yet had a woman President or Vice President. However, women have run for these offices. The first was Victoria Woodhull in 1872, a candidate of the Equal Rights party.

The President may be the most powerful person in the whole world. Some people say the job of the President is the hardest job there is. When things go well, the President is a popular leader. When they do not go well, he often gets most of the blame. In spite of the ups and downs, every four years there are many people who want to run for the office of President of the United States.

Abraham Lincoln was sworn in as President in 1861.

Laws and Facts About the Presidency

The Constitution says very little about who can be President. It simply tells us that the President must:

1. be born a citizen of the United States.

2. be over the age of 35.

3. have lived in the United States for at least 14 years.

The Constitution also states that the President's **term** of office shall be for four years. The Twenty-second Amendment to the Constitution puts a limit on the number of terms a President can serve. A person can be elected no more than two times.

History Fact

John F. Kennedy was the youngest person ever elected President. He was 43 years old. Ronald Reagan, at age 69, was the oldest person ever elected.

Congress decides the pay for the President. The last time the President got a pay raise was in 1969. At that time, the President's yearly pay was set at $200,000. The President also gets up to $119,000 a year for expenses.

The President lives and works in the White House. It is in the center of Washington, D.C., the nation's capital. The White House is a huge mansion with more than 130 rooms and offices. The President gets the use of cars, planes, boats, and helicopters. The President can also use Camp David, a vacation retreat in the mountains near Washington, for meetings and rest.

The Jobs of the President

The President is the head of the executive branch of the federal government. The job is not simple because it is a combination of many jobs. The President leads the country in at least six very important ways.

Chief Executive The Constitution gives the President power to carry out laws. As chief executive, the President picks people to help him run the government. He sends ideas for laws to the Congress, and he decides how to best carry out the laws Congress passes. He also must decide how to spend the government's money. Every year he makes a spending plan called a **budget**. Congress must approve the budget before the money can be spent.

Remember
The President makes the budget, but the Congress must approve it. This is an example of checks and balances.

The President heads one of the largest groups of departments in the world. He is the boss of more than three million government workers. The money spent in every department of the executive branch must fit within the budget. Every year, more than $1 trillion is spent under the executive branch.

Chief of State In this case, state is another name for country. In some countries, a king or queen handles the jobs that our President performs. The

In his role as Chief of State, President Clinton held summit meetings with various leaders from other countries.

President meets with visitors from other countries and gives speeches on important holidays. Meeting visitors and giving speeches are **ceremonial** jobs. The President represents the United States to the other countries of the world. As the nation's leading citizen, he is looked up to by all people in the country. The President must live up to the job he holds.

Chief Diplomat The President is also the nation's chief **diplomat**. He is responsible for setting the **foreign policy** of the country. The President decides what **treaties** to make with other nations. He appoints **ambassadors** to represent the United States in foreign countries. As chief diplomat, the President tries to keep the United States at peace with countries around the world.

Commander-in-Chief The President is the leader of the two million members of the armed forces. The President does not command the troops in the field. He is not even a member of the armed forces. However, the leaders of the army, navy, and air force take orders from him. The President has the power to send the armed forces anywhere in the world.

Government Fact

The President can send American troops anywhere in the world to protect U.S. interests. However, only Congress can declare war.

Chief Lawmaker Congress, of course, makes the laws. However, the President has much to do with which laws Congress passes. First of all, the President has the veto power. Second, the President often proposes laws to Congress. Sometimes he must work hard to get Congress to vote for his ideas. Under the Constitution, the President must give a speech to Congress each year. In it, he explains the needs and goals of the country. This speech is called the State of the Union Address.

Party Chief The President is clearly the leader of his political party. Some Presidents have belonged to the Republican party. Others have belonged to the Democratic party. A person cannot become President without support from members of his party all around the country. The President is usually a person who has held lower political offices. Most often, the President has worked hard for his party for many years. This work continues after he is elected. The President helps

President Bill Clinton delivers the last State of the Union Address of his presidency to members of his Cabinet and members of Congress.

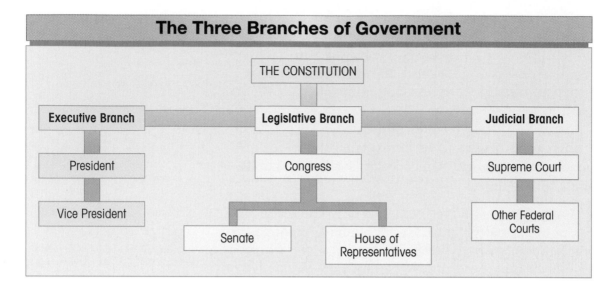

The Three Branches of Government

THE CONSTITUTION

Executive Branch — **Legislative Branch** — **Judicial Branch**

President | Congress | Supreme Court

Vice President | | Other Federal Courts

Senate | House of Representatives

other people in his party get elected to office. The President also works closely with the members of Congress who are in his party.

The President must do all of his jobs well. He must always put the best interests of the country first. At the same time, he must listen to and help all the people who helped elect him. This is especially true if he wishes to get reelected. This is why many people say being President is the toughest job in the world.

✔ Check Your Understanding

1. List the three qualifications the Constitution says a person must have to be President.

2. Choose three of the six major ways the President leads the country. Give a brief description of each.

The President's Team

Almost every day, the President must struggle with many problems. The President is the boss of more people than he can count. How does just one person handle such a huge job?

The President has many people who help get facts and give advice. The chart on page 90 shows the main groups or offices that make up the President's team. They are:

- the Vice President

- the White House Office

- the special councils

- the **Cabinet** (heads of the 14 executive departments)

The Vice President

In some ways, the Vice President should be the closest person to the President. He is elected to office along with the President. He is almost always chosen directly by the President to run for office with him.

However, the Vice President has far less power than the President. The Constitution gives him the job of leading the Senate. It also states that he would become the new President if the current President cannot do the job. This would happen if the President dies, becomes very ill, or leaves office for other reasons.

Since 1900, five Vice Presidents have succeeded to the presidency. Four of the Presidents died in office. The fifth President, Richard Nixon, was the only one to **resign**.

The President is the one who decides how much the Vice President will do. President George Bush gave Vice President Dan Quayle many important jobs. President Bill Clinton did the same thing with his Vice President, Al Gore. Today, most Presidents realize that the Vice President should be a key player on the executive team. That is the only way he can be fully prepared in case he has to become President in an emergency.

History Fact

The Vice President is said to be only "a heartbeat away" from the presidency. Nine of the 42 U.S. Presidents became President while serving as Vice President.

The Executive Office of the President

The President's top assistants work in the Executive Office of the President. The Executive Office is made up of several offices and **councils** staffed by some of the President's closest advisers. They work in the White House itself or in nearby buildings. The Executive Office was created by Congress in 1939. Each President since then has reorganized the office to fit his needs and wishes.

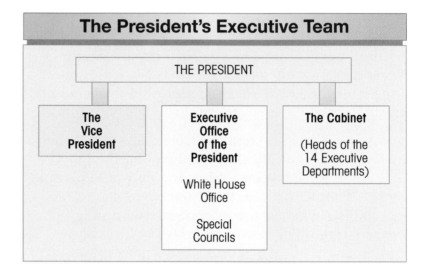

The President's Executive Team

THE PRESIDENT

The Vice President

Executive Office of the President

White House Office

Special Councils

The Cabinet

(Heads of the 14 Executive Departments)

The White House Office

The heart—or nerve center—of the Executive Office is the White House Office. The President's Chief-of-Staff directs the operations of this office and all the people who work in it. The White House Office advises the President daily about foreign policy, money matters, defense, and relations with Congress. Some of the people in the White House Office help to write the President's speeches. Others plan the President's trips. The President's press secretary is also a member of this White House staff. The press secretary's job is to give all the White House news to newspaper, TV, and radio reporters.

Special Councils

The President also gets help from a number of special councils within the Executive Office. These councils come up with different plans for the President to consider. One of the most important of these groups is the National Security Council (NSC). It makes plans for the security, or safety, of the country. This agency has the job of gathering information about the nation's security. It has agents stationed around the world. The National Security Council has only a few members. The Vice President, the Secretaries of State and Defense, the head of the Central Intelligence Agency (CIA), and a few other people make up the NSC.

Other special councils include the Office of Management and Budget (OMB), the Council of Economic Advisers, and the Council on Environmental Quality. The OMB prepares the yearly federal budget. Once the budget is approved by Congress, the OMB then keeps track of the spending of the funds. The OMB also studies how the executive branch is run. It can make suggestions for changes and improvements. The Council of Economic Advisers keeps a close watch on the nation's economy. The Council on Environmental Quality helps the President tackle the problems of keeping our **environment** clean and safe.

The Cabinet

Some of the President's closest advisers are the members of the Cabinet. The Cabinet is made up of the heads of the 14 executive departments. These officials serve two roles. They are responsible for all that goes on within their special departments. In addition, they all serve as close advisers to the President as experts in their special areas.

The Cabinet members are all called Secretaries, except for the head of the Justice Department. That department is headed by the Attorney General.

The President chooses each member of the Cabinet. However, the Senate has to approve his choices. Persons picked for the Cabinet usually have strong backgrounds in certain areas. For example, the Secretary of the Treasury has a lot of experience in finance. The Secretary of Agriculture knows a lot about farming and farm problems. The Secretary of Defense knows a lot about the military services and purchasing and building weapons.

The President holds Cabinet meetings about once or twice a week. The Secretaries report on what is happening within their departments. They also give the President advice in handling any problems. The Vice President and a few other officials of the executive branch attend these meetings. The meetings are closed to the press and public.

The President and the People

Through the departments and agencies of the executive branch, the President touches each of our lives every day. Yet the President remains the representative of the people of the United States. To carry out the presidency, the President must learn as much as possible about the country. The President must know what the people want from their government.

How does the President find out what the people want? The President listens to the White House Office staff. He hears what his Cabinet members have to say. He reads what newspapers write about him. He learns what the television news reports about him.

History Fact

President Franklin Roosevelt appointed Frances Perkins as Secretary of Labor in 1933. She was the first woman Cabinet member. In 1997, Madeleine Albright became the first woman to serve as Secretary of State.

All of this is important. Yet none of it is quite as important as knowing what the American public thinks. To be successful, a President must be popular. To be popular, the President needs to understand what the people think and want.

The President reads some of the letters that are sent to the White House. He also reads different studies that report how many people are for and against one matter or another. Above all, he travels all across the country talking to voters. He knows that his biggest job as President is to follow the will of the people.

✓ Check Your Understanding

1. What two roles does the Vice President fill under the Constitution?

2. Name one of the special councils to the President. Briefly describe its role.

Government Skills

PROFILING THE PRESIDENT

What did the President do before he took office? What experience does he bring to the job? What kinds of decisions can he be expected to make while in office? To get to know the President better, try making up a profile. A profile is a short set of facts about a person. The facts tell something about the person's life or background.

Copy the profile headings from the next page onto another piece of paper. Use the facts about President Abraham Lincoln to help you answer questions about our current President.

You can find most of these facts in the library. Some of the facts can be collected by reading or listening to the news. The White House Web site (www.whitehouse.gov) will give you biographical information about the President.

Profile of a President	
Name:	Abraham Lincoln
Birth date:	February 12, 1809
Birthplace:	Hodgenville, Kentucky
Home state:	Illinois
Family members:	wife: Mary Todd Lincoln; sons: Robert, Edward, William, Thomas
School background:	No formal education
Job before government work:	Lawyer
Political party:	Republican
Government jobs:	Member Illinois legislature (1834–1842); Member of House of Representatives (1847–1849)
Idea or law fought for in past:	Freed slaves with Emancipation Proclamation

For extra credit, make profiles of your senators and representative to Congress.

GOVERNMENT ISSUES
One Six-Year Term for the President?

Most Americans agree that the President's job is both important and difficult. Some people have even said that four years is too short a term for the office. Many Presidents have agreed. Some have asked for an amendment to the Constitution. They want the President to serve one six-year term. The idea for the six-year term has been before Congress many times before. However, each time, it has been killed.

People in favor of a one-term presidency say it would let the President serve the people better. He would have more time to get his programs passed through Congress. He could concentrate on his job without worrying about having to get reelected. He would always be free to do what is best for the country. He would not have to worry as much about what his political supporters want.

People against a one-term presidency say the system works best as it is now. They say that if a President knows he has to stand for reelection, he will work harder. He will stay more in touch with the wishes of the people. Furthermore, members of Congress will work *with* the President if they know he could be President for eight years.

To change the presidency to one six-year term would require a constitutional amendment. That is probably why the idea still does not have great support around the country. However, that can always change. Someday in the future, the American people may decide they do want a one-term presidency.

You Decide

Would our system of government be better off with a one-term, six-year presidency? Why or why not? What other reasons, aside from the ones listed on this page, can you give for your answer?

Summary

The President serves a four-year term and may be elected twice.
The President has six major jobs as the leader of the country: • Chief executive—heads a giant workforce that carries out the laws • Chief of state—meets with leaders of other nations • Chief diplomat—sets the country's foreign policy • Commander-in-chief—is the leader of the armed forces • Chief lawmaker—can propose laws to Congress and veto bills from Congress • Party chief—is the leader of his political party
The President's executive team is made up of the Vice President, the members of the Cabinet, the White House Office, and the special councils.
The Vice President has only two roles under the Constitution: the President of the Senate and successor to the presidency.
The Cabinet is made up of the heads of the 14 executive departments. They advise the President.
The special councils come up with different plans for the President to consider.

treaty

foreign policy

budget

environment

diplomat

Vocabulary Review

Complete each sentence with a term from the list.

1. The way countries act toward one another is dictated by their _____.

2. A _____ is a plan for how to spend money.

3. Our natural surroundings are part of the _____.

4. An agreement between two countries is called a _____.

5. A _____ works with people from other countries.

Chapter Quiz

Write your answers in complete sentences.

1. In which of his roles does the President prepare a budget?

2. In which of his roles does the President set the country's foreign policy?

3. If the President vetoes a bill, what role is he carrying out?

4. Who decides what jobs the Vice President is given besides his constitutional ones?

5. What government body has to approve the President's choices of Cabinet members?

6. **Critical Thinking** Which of the President's major jobs do you think is most important?

7. **Critical Thinking** Do you think the responsibilities of the President should be increased, decreased, or remain the same? Explain your answer.

Write About Government

Complete the following activity.

Choose a newspaper story about the President in one of his six major roles. Read the story carefully. Then answer the following questions.

1. What did the President do?

2. In which of his roles was he acting?

3. Did he get any advice or help from anyone on his executive team? Who?

4. Did he go to the American people for advice or support? How?

The Pentagon Building, headquarters of the Defense Department, is in Washington, D.C.

Learning Objectives

- Explain the background and history of the executive departments.
- Identify and describe the responsibilities of the 14 executive departments.
- Explain the background and history of the independent agencies.
- Identify and describe the responsibilities of some key independent agencies.

Words to Know

embassy	the office and official home of a country's ambassador
consulate	the official home of a *consul*; a consul is a government official sent to a foreign country to protect the home country's business interests and its citizens
customs duty	a government tax on imported goods
enforce	to make someone or something obey a rule or law
immigration	the act of entering and settling in a country not of one's birth
conservation	the act of keeping the natural environment safe and protected
patent	the official right given to an inventor to make or sell an invention for a certain time without being copied
administer	to manage or have charge of
veteran	a person who has served in the country's armed forces
independent agency	a government body or group that is free from control of the three branches of government
regulate	to control by rule or method
commerce	any trade or business activity
civilian	not involving the armed forces
bureaucracy	a large government organization made up of many offices and bureaus

The Beginnings of the Executive Departments

In 1789, the first Congress set up three executive departments: State, Treasury, and War. These three departments were established to help President George Washington run the executive branch. The position of Attorney General was also created then.

Over the years, the work of the federal government has increased. As a result, Congress has added new departments. Some departments have been combined, and others have been done away with. Today, there are 14 executive departments. Together, they employ millions of people all around the country.

Organization and Duties

Each executive department is organized along the same lines. The head of the department is called the Secretary. In the case of the Justice Department, the top official is the Attorney General. The department heads are all appointed by the President, but then they must be approved by the Senate.

Remember
Cabinet members serve as close advisers to the President. They are experts in their special areas.

The department heads have many roles. They are all members of the President's Cabinet. They advise the President and report on all the activities of their departments. They must see to it that their departments carry out the President's policies and programs. They also testify before Congress. They often seek more money for their departments at budget hearings. They ask for support for new programs. They may also be called as expert witnesses on proposed bills.

Each department head has a top assistant, called the under secretary or deputy secretary. Each department also has several assistant secretaries. The deputy and assistant secretaries are also named by the President and must be approved by the Senate.

Within each executive department, there are many smaller agencies. These agencies are called bureaus, offices, services, or divisions. Many of the assistant secretaries are in charge of these agencies. Although the main offices of the departments are in Washington, D.C., the agencies are spread throughout the country. In this way, they can serve the people better.

Most executive department employees are "career people." That means they continue to work for the departments for many years through many presidential administrations. The top people in the departments, from assistant secretaries up through the Secretary, are almost always replaced with each new President.

President Clinton is shown at one of his Cabinet meetings.

The 14 Executive Departments

A brief description of the functions and responsibilities of each executive department appears on the following pages.

Department of State Established: 1789
Responsibilities: Serves as the President's "right arm" in all foreign relations. Advises President and helps carry out President's foreign policy. Manages U.S. **embassies** and **consulates** around the world. Protects American citizens who work or travel in foreign countries.

Major Agencies: Bureau of European Affairs; Bureau of Economic and Business Affairs; Bureau of Consular Affairs

Department of Treasury Established: 1789
Responsibilities: Collects taxes and **customs duties.** Borrows and repays money for federal government. Prints and coins money. Manages the national banks.

Major Agencies: Internal Revenue Service; U.S. Customs Service; U.S. Secret Service

Department of Interior Established: 1849
Responsibilities: Manages more than 500 million acres of public land. Plans **conservation,** development, and use of natural and wildlife resources. Manages national park system and American Indian reservations.

Major Agencies: Bureau of Land Management; National Park Service; Bureau of Indian Affairs

Department of Justice Established: 1870
Responsibilities: Gives legal advice to President and heads of other executive departments. Represents the United States in court cases. **Enforces** federal criminal laws, federal civil rights, antitrust, and immigration laws. Manages the federal prison system.

Major Agencies: Federal Bureau of Investigation (FBI); Civil Rights Division; **Immigration** and Naturalization Service; Drug Enforcement Administration

Department of Agriculture Established: 1889

Responsibilities: Helps the nation's farmers plan and use the best farming methods. Inspects and grades meat, poultry, and dairy products. Runs national school lunch programs for students from low-income families.

Major Agencies: Farmers Home Administration; Food and Safety Inspection Service; Agricultural Research Service

Department of Commerce Established: 1913

Responsibilities: Promotes and encourages trade between the United States and other countries. Helps the country's economy grow. Gathers information about the U.S. population through census taking. Protects inventors of new products and ideas by issuing **patents.**

Major Agencies: International Trade Administration; Bureau of Census; Patent and Trademark Office; National Weather Service

Department of Labor Established: 1913

Responsibilities: Enforces federal labor laws, such as those of minimum wages and child labor. Provides benefits to workers and the unemployed. Publishes information about wages, prices, living conditions, and size of the work force. Sets health and safety standards.

Major Agencies: Employment and Training Administration; Occupational Safety and Health Administration; Bureau of Labor Statistics

Department of Defense Established: 1949 (Combined War and Navy departments by act of Congress)

Responsibilities: Controls the nation's armed forces (army, navy, air force). Advises President on all military and national security matters. Supervises the improvement of nation's rivers and harbors.

Government Fact

A census is an official count of a country's population. A "census taker" usually gathers information about the age, race, sex, and occupation of the population.

Major Agencies: The Department of the Army; the Department of the Navy; the Department of the Air Force; the Army Corps of Engineers

Department of Housing and Urban Development (HUD) Established: 1965

Responsibilities: Provides help to U.S. cities in area of housing. Gives financial aid to cities to repair buildings and construct new housing. Also helps local governments repair water and sewer systems, and fight air pollution.

Major Agencies: HUD is one of three executive departments where programs are **administered** directly by assistant secretaries rather than by agencies. Assistant Secretary for Community Planning and Development; Assistant Secretary for Housing; Assistant Secretary for Public and Indian Housing

Department of Transportation Established: 1966

Responsibilities: Enforces federal laws on air, sea, rail, and highway safety. Operates and maintains the national highway and railroad systems. Provides financial help to state and local governments to build and develop their bus and rail systems.

Major Agencies: Federal Aviation Administration; U.S. Coast Guard; Federal Highway Administration; National Highway Traffic Safety Administration

Department of Energy Established: 1977

Responsibilities: To find, protect, and conserve the country's sources of energy—water power, oil, and natural gas. Also regulates the use of nuclear power.

Major Agencies: Programs administered directly by assistant secretaries. Assistant Secretary, Conservation and Renewable Energy; Assistant Secretary, Defense Programs; Assistant Secretary, Nuclear Energy

Department of Education Established: 1979 (formerly part of Department of Health, Education, and Welfare)

A teacher directs a Head Start class. Head Start is under the control of the Department of Education, which provides financial help for all levels of education.

Responsibilities: Provides financial help for all levels of education. Administers various programs to aid local and state governments for elementary schools, high schools, and colleges. Provides aid for programs for handicapped, disadvantaged, and gifted students as well. Publishes information and statistics about schools.

Major Agencies: Programs administered directly by assistant secretaries. Assistant Secretary for Elementary and Secondary Education; Assistant Secretary for Special Education and Rehabilitative Services; Assistant Secretary for Education Research and Improvement

Department of Health and Human Services
Established: 1979 (formerly part of Department of Health, Education, and Welfare)

Responsibilities: Manages several health and welfare programs for all Americans. Provides social security benefits to retired workers. Also provides aid to handicapped people. Conducts medical research.

Major Agencies: Social Security Administration; Health Care Financing Administration; Public Health Service

Department of Veterans Affairs Established: 1988; formerly the Veterans Administration

Responsibilities: Operates various programs to benefit **veterans** and their families. Provides financial help for education, medical care, and home loan purchases.

Major Agencies: Veterans Benefits Administration; Veterans Health Services and Research Administration; National Cemetery System

✓ **Check Your Understanding**

1. What were the three original executive departments set up by the first Congress?

2. Describe two roles the department heads have.

3. Choose two executive departments, and briefly describe their responsibilities.

The Independent Agencies and Commissions

More than 100 years ago, Congress created the first **independent agency,** the Interstate Commerce Commission (ICC). The ICC was established to

regulate business between the nation's railroads and the people using them to transport goods.

Today, the federal government has more than 70 independent agencies. These agencies handle matters that fall outside the three branches of government. The President appoints the heads of these agencies. The Senate must approve these appointments. Congress must also approve all the budgets for these agencies. Aside from that, they are free from the control of the executive and legislative branches. Their decisions must always be lawful, however.

These independent agencies fall into two main groups. Many agencies are set up to administer programs that serve the American public. Some, such as the ICC, are regulatory commissions. That means they have the power to set rules and regulations about the activities they manage. They can also enforce their rules and regulations.

Here is a brief description of the functions and responsibilities of some of the most well-known and important agencies.

Environmental Protection Agency (EPA)
Established: 1970

The EPA's job is to protect the country's environment. The United States has become a very crowded country. The land, air, and water are in constant danger from misuse and pollution. Giant industries are often careless about the way they treat our natural resources. The EPA enforces the laws that Congress has passed to keep our air and water clean and free from pollution.

The Space Shuttle Columbia *was the first such space vehicle to be launched by NASA.*

National Aeronautics and Space Administration (NASA) Established: 1958

NASA is the agency in charge of America's space program. Its scientists and engineers have put space satellites and rockets into orbit around the earth and sent astronauts to the moon. Today, NASA operates the space shuttle program. Astronauts go into orbit and return to Earth in the same vehicle. NASA research programs have also made contributions to industry and medicine.

United States Postal Service Established: 1971

The Post Office runs the nation's mail system. It has the power to enforce the country's laws concerning mail delivery. For example, it is illegal to send certain items, such as guns and alcohol, through the mails.

Before 1971, the Post Office was an executive department. Today, it operates like a private business. Congress made it an independent agency in the hope that it would run more efficiently. If the Postal Service loses money, Congress helps pay for its costs.

The Postmaster General is the head of the service. The President appoints the Postmaster General and the board of nine governors. The Senate must approve these appointments.

ACTION Established: 1971

ACTION is an "umbrella" agency. That is, it organizes and supervises many of the government volunteer programs. Two of the most well-known ACTION programs are the Peace Corps and VISTA.

The Peace Corps was set up in 1961 to help develop friendly relations between the United States and other countries. Peace Corps volunteers are trained as teachers, engineers, farmers, and at a variety of other jobs. Then they are sent to areas of foreign countries where their skills can be put to best use.

VISTA is a short name for Volunteers in Service to America. Volunteers in this program help the more needy people in this country. These volunteers work with disadvantaged youths in inner city neighborhoods, house-bound senior citizens, and with Native Americans on their reservations.

Government Fact

An *umbrella* agency is one that covers several other agencies or programs.

Interstate Commerce Commission (ICC)
Established: 1887

Although the ICC was established to regulate railroads, today it does much more than that. It regulates all **commerce** carried on between states, whether by trains, trucks, buses, or boats. The ICC issues licenses for companies to operate. The companies must also get ICC approval for the rates they charge. The commission also sets safety rules which the companies must obey.

Federal Trade Commission (FTC) Established: 1914

The FTC was established to prevent unfair trading practices in business. The commission enforces laws against price fixing, false labeling, and untrue claims in advertising. The commission also checks products for safety before they are put on the market.

Federal Communications Commission (FCC)
Established: 1934

The FCC regulates the use of all radio and television stations around the country. It decides which stations can have a license to broadcast. It does not control the content of the programs that are broadcast. The commission also decides who can use the communications satellites that travel around the earth. The FCC also regulates telephone and telegraph rates between the states.

Consumer Product Safety Commission
Established: 1972

This commission's responsibility is to protect consumers from unsafe products that can cause illness, injury, or even death. The commission sets and enforces safety standards for more than 10,000 manufactured goods. It regulates the standards for a variety of products including appliances, baby clothes, sports equipment, and toys.

Nuclear Regulatory Commission (NRC)

Established: 1975

The NRC licenses and regulates all **civilian** nuclear power plants and all civilian use of nuclear materials. The commission's basic job is to see that nuclear power is used peacefully and safely. It also conducts research to find new and safer ways of using nuclear power.

The Nuclear Regulatory Commission sets rules for nuclear power plants, such as this one at Three Mile Island in Pennsylvania.

✓ **Check Your Understanding**

1. In what ways are the independent agencies under some control by the executive and legislative branches?

2. Name one service agency and one regulatory commission. Briefly describe their functions.

The Federal Bureaucracy

Together, the President's executive team, the executive departments, and the independent agencies make up the federal **bureaucracy.** The chart below shows where the various groups fit in this bureaucracy.

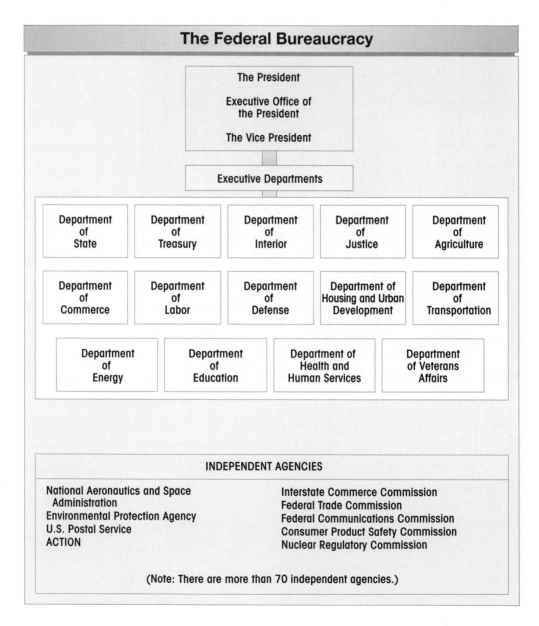

The Federal Bureaucracy

The President

Executive Office of the President

The Vice President

Executive Departments

Department of State	Department of Treasury	Department of Interior	Department of Justice	Department of Agriculture
Department of Commerce	Department of Labor	Department of Defense	Department of Housing and Urban Development	Department of Transportation
Department of Energy	Department of Education	Department of Health and Human Services	Department of Veterans Affairs	

INDEPENDENT AGENCIES

National Aeronautics and Space Administration
Environmental Protection Agency
U.S. Postal Service
ACTION

Interstate Commerce Commission
Federal Trade Commission
Federal Communications Commission
Consumer Product Safety Commission
Nuclear Regulatory Commission

(Note: There are more than 70 independent agencies.)

GOVERNMENT ISSUES
Foreign Aid

The United States is a rich country. Over the past 50 years, our country has given a lot of help to other countries. The help might consist of food, money, bank loans, or military goods. This help to other countries is called *foreign aid*. An independent agency called AID (Agency for International Development) is in charge of most of the foreign aid. AID works closely with the State Department to deal with the leaders of other countries. For food aid, it works through the Department of Agriculture. Military aid is given through the Department of Defense.

Since the 1950s, most U.S. foreign aid has gone to countries in Asia and Latin America. Many of those countries have large numbers of people who need food. They need much better housing, schooling, and medical care.

Much of the money to these countries is lent to them. The idea was that once the countries began to make economic progress, they could pay back the loans. However, things have not always worked out that way. Many of these countries continue to have serious problems. Some cannot pay back the loans. In 1999, it was suggested that these loans be forgiven. This means that the loans would not have to be paid back.

Many Americans think we should continue to help the less fortunate nations in the world. However, not all agree. Many people think we should stop giving so much aid to other countries. They ask, "How can we give away billions of dollars? We have many homeless, sick, and hungry people right here in the United States."

The United States will probably continue giving foreign aid for years to come. Government leaders agree that the United States cannot turn its back on the starving and sick people in other nations.

You Decide

Should this country continue to give large amounts of foreign aid to other nations? Or should this country use the money on problems at home? Give reasons for your answer.

Summary

The first Congress created three executive departments: State, Treasury, and War. Today, there are 14 departments. The heads of the executive departments are called secretaries.
The executive departments contain smaller agencies called bureaus, offices, services, or divisions.
The federal government also has more than 70 independent agencies. These agencies handle matters that fall outside the three branches of government.
The independent agencies fall into two groups. Many agencies administer programs that serve the people. Some agencies are regulatory commissions.

Vocabulary Review

Write *true* or *false*. If the statement is false, change the underlined word to make it true.

1. <u>Patents</u> keep the environment protected.

2. When people move to live in a different country than the one in which they were born, it is called <u>immigration</u>.

3. A <u>civilian</u> is not a part of the armed forces.

4. An <u>embassy</u> is the official home of a consul.

5. A <u>customs duty</u> is a tax on goods from another country.

Chapter Quiz

Write your answers in complete sentences.

1. What are two responsibilities of the Department of State?

2. What are two responsibilities of the Department of Justice?

3. What are two responsibilities of the Department of Energy?

4. What are two responsibilities of the Department of Transportation?

5. What was the first independent agency created by Congress? What are the responsibilities of the agency today?

6. What is the role of the regulatory commissions?

7. **Critical Thinking** Why is ACTION called an "umbrella" agency?

8. **Critical Thinking** Why do you think the executive department heads would testify before Congress?

Write About Government

Complete the following activity.

Make a chart showing any two of the executive departments. Draw a box with the name of the department in it. Then draw connecting lines down to three boxes with the names of three of the department's bureaus or divisions. Inside the three boxes, list responsibilities of the bureaus or divisions.

The nine justices of the Supreme Court are shown here.

Learning Objectives

- Identify the kinds of cases handled by the federal court system.

- Explain the role and responsibilities of the U.S. District Courts.

- Explain the role and responsibilities of the U.S. Courts of Appeals.

- Explain the role and responsibilities of the U.S. Supreme Court.

- Identify and describe two important Supreme Court cases that show how our laws can change.

Words to Know

guilty	judged to have done something wrong or against the law
innocent	judged not to have done something against the law
criminal case	involving a crime, a breaking of the law
civil case	involving a disagreement over private rights
jury	in civil or criminal cases, the people chosen to decide the case
sentence	punishment set by a court of law for a crime, such as a jail term or fine
appeal	to ask a higher court to review a lower court's decision; *appellate* means having to do with an appeal
jurisdiction	power or authority
review	to look over; to examine once more
uphold	maintain or support
overturn	to throw out or turn over
majority opinion	a written statement giving reasons for a Supreme Court ruling
dissenting opinion	a written statement giving reasons for disagreeing with a Supreme Court ruling
public	anything that is run by the government and open to everyone (such as public schools)
legal	having to do with the law; acts that are within the law
segregate	to separate people or groups from each other

The Federal Court System

Article III of the Constitution established the third branch of the government, the judicial branch. The judicial branch is made up of all the federal courts in the country. At the top of this system is the U.S. Supreme Court. It is the nation's most powerful court.

The Constitution established only one court—the Supreme Court. However, it gave Congress the power to establish lower federal courts. Today, the federal system consists of district courts, courts of appeals, and the Supreme Court. There are also special courts that decide cases involving trade, taxes, and military matters.

Our system of law says that when a person is accused of a crime, he or she is brought before a court. Then a judge and a jury will decide if the person is **guilty** or **innocent.** The Constitution says that a person is innocent of a crime until proven guilty. Furthermore, that proof must be made in a court of law.

Most **criminal cases** are heard in state courts. That is because they involve the breaking of state laws. The federal courts handle only three main kinds of cases.

1. Cases dealing with the Constitution Federal courts handle questions about the meaning of the Constitution. They also decide cases about a person or group that may have done something that is against the Constitution.

2. Cases dealing with federal laws Federal courts decide all cases that have to do with laws passed by Congress. Some of these cases involve people who break tax laws, mail laws, or banking laws.

3. Cases dealing with more than one state Some cases deal with people or laws from more than one state. Federal courts handle these cases.

United States District Courts

The lowest federal courts are the district courts. There are 91 of these courts spread across the United States. Each state has at least one, and some have as many as four. Most federal cases begin in the district courts.

The district courts are the federal trial courts. People accused of such crimes as bank robbery, kidnapping, and breaking tax laws are tried there. These courts also hear federal **civil cases.** These cases involve some disagreement over a contract, relations between businesses, or other noncriminal cases.

Each district has at least one judge, but many have several. The court cases are usually heard by a single judge. Certain cases are heard by a three-judge panel. In some cases, the judge decides who wins the case. In other cases, a **jury** of twelve people from the area decides who wins. In both cases, the judge decides what the **sentence** is if someone is found guilty.

United States Courts of Appeals

Sometimes, people think they did not get a fair trial in district court. They think the judge was unfair or the trial did not follow the rules. What can they do?

These people have a right to **appeal.** They can ask a higher court to hear the case. The United States Courts of Appeals are the next higher federal courts. These courts are spread across the United States in 11 large judicial areas called circuits. There is one U.S. Court of Appeals in each circuit and one for the District of Columbia.

Congress established the Courts of Appeals in 1891. They were set up to relieve the Supreme Court from hearing so many appeals from the district courts. The 12 Courts of Appeals usually hear appeals from the

Remember
The Constitution gives Congress the power to establish federal courts.

district courts within their circuits. The circuit courts have only appellate **jurisdiction.** This means they cannot try cases. They can only hear appeals.

The number of judges on each circuit court varies from 3 to 15. A minimum of three judges on any court hears a case. Sometimes, for a very important case, all the judges in a circuit may hear the appeal.

If a court of appeals decides to **review** a case, the judges first study its history. They listen to lawyers for both sides. The judges also check the written records from the district court. They check to see that the lawyers, the judge, and the jury of the lower court all followed court laws.

If the judges decide that all the laws were followed correctly, the lower court decision is **upheld.** If the judges find that a mistake was made or that the trial was not fair, the lower court decision is **overturned.** The case goes back to district court for a new trial.

✓ **Check Your Understanding**

1. What are the three kinds of cases the federal courts handle?

2. Where do most federal cases begin?

United States Supreme Court

The final court of appeals in the country is the United States Supreme Court. It is the highest court in the nation. The Court makes the final decision whether a law or an act is unconstitutional. The Court decides the meaning of the Constitution.

The Supreme Court has both original and appellate jurisdiction. That means it can hear cases brought directly to it or review cases on appeal from lower

This is the Supreme Court building in Washington, D.C. Every year, the justices meet here from October to June.

courts. The Court has the authority to hear two kinds of cases in original jurisdiction. One type is a case that involves a state. The other is a case that involves an ambassador or a consul.

Most of the cases the Court hears are appeals from lower federal courts or state supreme courts. The Supreme Court decides itself whether or not it will review a case on appeal. Each year, some 4,500 cases are appealed to the Court. However, the Court will usually only accept a few hundred to review.

The judges of the Supreme Court are called justices. There are eight associate justices and a Chief Justice on the Court. The justices are appointed by the President. However, the appointments must be approved by the Senate. Supreme Court justices—like district and courts of appeals judges—are appointed for life. Many justices serve for years, some for decades.

Hearing the Cases

The Supreme Court holds its sessions each year from early October until the following June. All the justices

History Fact

William O. Douglas served the longest term of any Supreme Court Justice—36 years (1939–1975).

are present when a case is heard. Lawyers from both sides are given a certain amount of time to present their cases. The justices often question the lawyers during this time. The lawyers also supply written briefs to the Court to further support their cases.

The Court generally hears cases for a period of two weeks. Then, the justices study the cases for another two-week period called a recess. The Court's continuing term is made up of two weeks of hearing cases followed by two weeks of recesses.

Deciding the Cases

Before deciding a case, the justices study the written briefs. They review the important facts of the case. They also read about earlier cases that may have involved similar points of law. They want to know what other judges have decided in the past about such cases.

Finally, the justices meet alone in a room to vote. Six of the justices must be present before a vote can be taken. Each justice gives his or her views on the case. The judges question each other carefully. Sometimes, they argue with each other. After each justice has spoken, a vote is taken.

If the vote on a case is 9–0, it is called a *unanimous decision*. If the vote goes any other way, such as 6–3 or 5–4, then the Court has reached a *split decision*. Whatever the vote, the decision is final.

Shortly after the vote, it is decided who will write the opinions on the case. One justice is assigned the **majority opinion**. This opinion will state the reasons why the Court decided the way it did. In a split decision, one justice from the minority will be assigned to write the **dissenting opinion**. That opinion will explain the views of the justices who voted against the decision. Before they are made

public, these opinions are passed back and forth among the other justices. They are free to add their own comments.

Supreme Court opinions are studied very closely. Lawyers, judges, and **legal** experts around the country read them carefully. These opinions often are used by lower court judges to decide cases that are similar to the ones decided by the Supreme Court. In addition, the opinions are used by future Supreme Court justices to help them decide their own cases.

Our Changing Laws

Since its beginnings, the Supreme Court has decided thousands and thousands of cases. Many cases have shaped our laws and the way we understand our Constitution. However, times change, and so do ideas. Sometimes, the Court changes its mind about an earlier decision. This happened with two cases concerning the rights of African Americans.

The First Decision One day in 1892, an African American named Homer Plessy got on a train in New Orleans, Louisiana. In those days, some state laws set aside different railroad cars for African Americans and for whites. Plessy took a seat in a car marked "For Whites Only." He was arrested for breaking the law. However, Plessy believed that such laws violated the Constitution.

Plessy's case was heard in the Louisiana state courts. He lost. Then Plessy appealed to the United States Supreme Court. The Court took the case because it brought up an important question about the Constitution. The Fourteenth Amendment promised all people equal protection under state laws. Did the Louisiana state law take away the rights promised to Plessy by the Fourteenth Amendment?

In 1896, the Supreme Court upheld the lower court decision. It ruled that the Louisiana law was

History Fact

These state laws involved more than railroad cars. In some states, there were separate parks, schools, hotels, restaurants, and even drinking fountains for African Americans and whites.

constitutional as long as the "Blacks Only" railroad car was just as good as all other railroad cars. The Court ruled in *Plessy* v. *Ferguson* that the law did not violate the Fourteenth Amendment. It said that the railroad cars were separate but equal. For decades, other states used this ruling to **segregate** African Americans and whites in many other areas.

The Second Decision In the 1950s, some African American parents in Topeka, Kansas, tested these laws again. They believed that the schools for their children were not as good as the Topeka schools for white children. Like Homer Plessy, these parents lost their case in the state courts. Just as in the *Plessy* case, they appealed to the United States Supreme Court.

The year was 1954, almost 60 years since the Supreme Court's ruling on Homer Plessy's case. Both the Supreme Court justices and many people in the country had changed their ideas about what was fair and right. In *Brown* v. *Board of Education of Topeka,* the Supreme Court ruled unanimously that separate public schools for African Americans and for whites went against the Constitution. The Court said that the separate but equal rule had "no place" in the field of public education. Over time, the Court would rule that segregation by race was unconstitutional in all other areas as well. This decision shows that the Supreme Court can change the law as times change.

Other Special Courts

Over the years, Congress has created several other federal courts. These courts hear special cases that fall outside the jurisdiction of the federal district courts. Here are some special courts and their responsibilities.

United States Claims Court Hears cases in which someone has a financial claim against the U.S. government. A person who sues the government and wins is entitled to collect money.

In the 1950s, federal law ordered integration in the schools. These students in Little Rock, Arkansas, are shown being protected by Federal troops in December 1957.

The Territorial Courts Hear cases involving people who live in the U.S. territories—Guam, the Virgin Islands, and the Mariana Islands.

The Court of Military Appeals Hears appeals from members of the armed forces who have been found guilty of military crimes.

United States Tax Court Hears noncriminal cases concerning the payment of federal taxes. Settles disputes over the amount of taxes to be paid.

The Court of International Trade Hears cases involving tariffs and other trade-related laws.

✓ **Check Your Understanding**

1. What two kinds of cases can the Supreme Court hear under original jurisdiction?

2. Describe what happens when the Supreme Court justices gather to vote on a case.

3. Who decides who will write the opinions in the cases decided by the Court?

LANDMARK CHANGES IN THE LAW
Freedom of Speech

The Constitution's First Amendment protects the right of all people to speak their thoughts freely. Does that mean all words are protected at all times? During World War I, Congress outlawed any speaking out against the U.S. government when it would hurt the nation's security.

One man, named Schenck, tried to talk thousands of men into resisting the draft. Avoiding military service was against the law. Schenck was arrested. In court, he was found to have broken the law. Schenck appealed his case to the Supreme Court. He said Congress's law was unconstitutional. It did not protect his right to speak freely.

In 1919, the Supreme Court heard his case, *Schenck* v. *United States*. The Court decided that the law did not go against the Constitution. Congress had a need to protect the country during the dangers of wartime. Justice Oliver Wendell Holmes wrote the decision. He said that all people have the right to speak freely. However, if a person's words create a "clear and present danger," then Congress has a right to outlaw them. For example, if someone yells "Fire!" in a crowded theater (when there is really no fire), it would probably cause a panic. People could be hurt or killed. The First Amendment does not protect such words in those circumstances.

When speaking freely becomes a danger to others, it may not be protected by the Constitution. Over many years and in many cases, the Supreme Court has decided such points about the meanings of the Constitution.

You Decide

Was the Supreme Court right in saying that Congress could stop Mr. Schenck from speaking out against the government in wartime? Explain.

Supreme Court Justice Oliver Wendell Holmes served from 1902 to 1932.

Government Skills

READING LEGAL CASE NAMES

Law cases are court battles between two people or between a person and the government. The name of each case tells who was arguing with whom. The case you read about on page 126 was *Schenck* v. *United States.* The first name listed, *Schenck,* tells who brought the case to court. The *v.* stands for the word *versus,* which means "against." The second name listed tells the party against whom the case was brought. When you read the case name, you say, "Schenck against the United States."

The case you read about on page 124 was called *Brown* v. *Board of Education of Topeka.* In what year was the case decided? Who won that case? Who lost the case?

Summary

The Constitution established the third branch of government, the judicial branch. The judicial branch is made up of all the federal courts in the country.
The federal court system consists of district courts, courts of appeals, and the Supreme Court.
The lowest federal courts are the 91 district courts. These courts are the federal trial courts.
The U.S. Courts of Appeals are the next higher federal courts. These 12 courts are spread across the United States in judicial areas called *circuits.*
The United States Supreme Court is the highest court in the nation. It decides the meaning of the Constitution.
Congress has created several special federal courts to hear certain kinds of cases.

jury
legal
sentence
innocent
dissenting opinion

Vocabulary Review

Write the term from the list that matches the definition below.

1. Pertaining to the law

2. Someone who has not committed a crime

3. A statement against the ruling of the Supreme Court

4. A group of people that make decisions about the law

5. A punishment given to someone who has broken the law

Chapter Quiz

Write your answers in complete sentences.

1. How many district courts are there in the federal court system?

2. What kind of civil cases do the district courts hear?

3. What does it mean when a federal court has only *appellate* jurisdiction?

4. What does it mean when a lower court decision is *upheld?*

5. What happens when a lower court decision is *overturned?*

6. Who decides whether or not the Supreme Court will review a case?

7. Critical Thinking Supreme Court justices should be appointed to serve for a period of years, not for life. Explain why you agree or disagree with this statement.

8. Critical Thinking Is it a good policy for there to be a dissenting opinion in a Supreme Court decision? Explain.

Write About Government

Complete the following activities.

1. Briefly describe the issues involved in the 1896 Supreme Court decision, *Plessy* v. *Ferguson.* What were the similarities to the 1954 case, *Brown* v. *Board of Education of Topeka?* What were the differences? What did the Court decide in the second case? How did that affect the first case?

2. In the case *Schenck* v. *United States,* the Supreme Court put some limits on the right of free speech. In your own words, briefly describe what "clear and present danger" means.

Unit 2 **Review**

Comprehension Check

Complete the sentences by choosing the correct word or phrase.

1. In the U.S. Senate, (each state has two votes/large states have more votes than small states).

2. In the U.S. House of Representatives, members serve (six-year/two-year) terms.

3. In all cases, for a bill to become law it (must pass both houses of Congress/must be proposed by the President).

4. The U.S. Constitution limits the President to (one six-year term/two four-year terms).

5. As the leader of the armed forces, the President is filling his role as (chief executive/commander-in-chief).

6. The groups that come up with plans for the President to consider are the (special councils/independent agencies).

7. The groups that set rules and regulations for the activities they manage are the (executive departments/regulatory commissions).

8. When the Supreme Court issues a ruling that all the justices agree on, then the Court has reached a (unanimous/split) decision.

Writing an Essay

Answer one of the following essay topics.

1. Summarize the separation of powers and the responsibilities of each of the three branches of American government.

2. Explain how a bill becomes a law.

3. Explain the roles and responsibilities of the President of the United States in the legislative and judicial branches of government.

Government in Your Life
Who are the two United States senators from your state? Are they Democrats or Republicans? Explain how their party allegiance affects their voting.

Unit 3

State and Local Government

Chapter 10

The Powers of the States

The state capitol building in Hartford, Connecticut, is shown in the photo above.

Learning Objectives

- Explain why the states need their own governments.
- Describe the limits on the states' power.
- Describe the powers reserved for the states.
- Identify the ways the state constitutions are like the U.S. Constitution.
- Describe the general powers of the states.
- Describe the ways that states work with the federal government.

Words to Know

alliance	a union of nations joined in a common cause
reserved	set aside or saved for a special reason
illegal	against the law
federal aid	money that the federal government gives to the states

The Need for State Governments

The United States is one of the largest countries in the world. It stretches almost 3,000 miles from Maine to California. The distance from the tip of Texas to the northern part of Alaska is almost 7,000 miles. Hawaii sits out in the Pacific Ocean, many thousands of miles from the other states. It is no wonder that there are many differences among the 50 states.

There are mountain states, plains states, desert states, and coastal states. There are states with a few hundred thousand people and others with several million. In some states, many of the people are farmers. In others, most are miners, ranchers, or factory workers. Michigan is known for making cars. Florida is known for growing oranges. Maine is famous for its fishing. Each state has something special about it.

It is easy to see why the federal government alone cannot handle the special needs of each state. The country is too big for that. That is why every state has its own government.

Each state government makes its own state laws to take care of its own needs. Connecticut may have special laws about air conditioning in public buildings.

Minnesota may have special laws about hunting and fishing. Ohio may want more land for state parks. California may want more land for housing or farming.

A state government takes care of needs like these. The federal government lets each state solve its own problems. This allows the federal government to take care of things that are important to the people of all the states.

Limiting the States' Powers

Remember
The document that established the first U.S. government was the Articles of Confederation. It was replaced by the Constitution.

Before the Constitution was written, the original 13 states had many powers that only the federal government has today. Some states coined their own money. They taxed goods that came from other states. They tried raising their own armies. Each state wanted to do things its own way. This led to fighting between the states. A strong federal government was needed to settle the problems between the states. That is why the Constitution was written. The men who attended the Constitutional Convention knew the United States needed a stronger central government in order to survive as a nation.

The Maryland state legislature meets every year in Annapolis, the state capital.

Article I, Section 10 of the Constitution spells out the powers that are denied to the states. Among the things states may not do are:

- enter into any treaty, **alliance**, or confederation.

- print or coin money.

- grant titles of nobility.

- engage in war with a foreign power or raise armies.

In addition, over the years amendments have been added to the Constitution that deny certain powers to the states.

Although the Constitution created a strong federal government, it still **reserved** many powers for the states. The states have the powers to:

- establish local governments.

- establish schools.

- run all local and state elections.

- set laws for marriage and divorce.

- issue licenses for certain types of workers to practice within the state. These workers could be doctors, lawyers, plumbers, barbers, and so on.

State Constitutions

To do its job properly, a state government needs a set of written laws. That is why every state has a state constitution. Its constitution is the highest law in that state.

All state constitutions follow the U.S. Constitution in four basic ways.

1. Rule by the people The people of each state control their government by electing their leaders.

Government Fact

Amendments 13, 14, 15, 19, 24, and 26 place limits on state powers.

2. **Limited government** The state governments have limited powers. All rights and freedoms protected in the Bill of Rights must be protected at the state level.

3. **Separation of powers** The state governments are divided into three branches: legislative, executive, and judicial.

4. **Checks and balances** The state constitutions provide for a system of checks and balances within the three government branches.

✓ **Check Your Understanding**

   1. Why is it necessary for each state to have its own government?

   2. What kinds of powers did the original 13 states have that only the federal government has today?

   3. Name at least three powers the Constitution denies to the states.

The States' Powers

   A state constitution lists the powers that the state has within its own borders. Each state has the power to pass laws and make sure that people follow them. Each state can set up courts for dealing with people who break the laws. A state can raise money by borrowing it or by taxing the people. It can make rules for doing business within the state. Each state also has a general power to protect the health, safety, and well-being of its people.

Health A state guards its people's health in many ways. It sets rules and regulations for restaurants, public swimming pools, theaters, sports arenas, and other public places. These rules can concern everything from the cleanliness of restaurant kitchens to smoking and nonsmoking sections in theaters. States also have the power to pass laws about air pollution, the drinking age, and the sale of **illegal** drugs.

Safety A state guards its people's safety in many ways, too. It can set highway speed limits and safety rules for workers. It can make rules for building safe houses. It can pass laws about owning and carrying guns. In addition, it can take steps to fight crime.

One of the powers of the states is to protect the safety of the people through law enforcement.

Well-Being Sometimes, a state will limit the people's rights in order to protect the public's well-being. A state can set the age for learning to drive or for getting married. It can say who must go to school and what must be taught. A state can give tests to lawyers, doctors, and other people who work within the state. This is to make sure they know how to do their jobs well. The state can also set business hours for bars and make laws about gambling.

Normally, a state can pass any law that is necessary for the well-being of its people. However, a state law cannot violate the U.S. Constitution. If it does, the law can be declared unconstitutional. This happened in 1962 in New York, Pennsylvania, and Maryland. These states passed laws that said every public school should start the day with a prayer. However, the U.S. Supreme Court ruled that these laws went against the Constitution. The Court said these laws were not in keeping with the First Amendment right to freedom of religion. As a result of that decision, the laws were thrown out.

Working with the Federal Government

Most of the time, state and federal governments work separately. However, there are times when they work together to solve a state or a national problem.

One such problem the country faces is air pollution. Almost every state has to deal with air made dirty by factories and cars. Suppose only one state tried to do something about it. One state alone could not do much good if its neighboring states did nothing. In order to clean up the air, many states have to work together.

Many states receive aid from the federal government to help pay for operating mass transit systems. Pictured here is a Boston, Massachusetts, subway platform.

To encourage this effort, the federal government gives states **federal aid.** Federal aid is money provided to states to help solve a national problem such as air pollution. The federal government sets rules about how clean the air has to be in each state. Then it gives each state money—in some cases up to millions of dollars. The money has to be spent to see that the law is carried out.

Each state may use the money in a different way to clean up its air. Pennsylvania may want to clean up air pollution from factories. California might use its federal money to clean up pollution from cars. New York might want to spend its money on new trains.

You Decide

Why do you think
the federal
government lets
the states decide
how to spend
federal aid money?

Federal aid is also given to the states for other reasons. For example, the federal government helps the states pay for the costs of state education. The states also get financial help in building and improving their highways and rail and bus systems. The states must follow federal rules and guidelines in using this money.

The federal government also helps the states when a natural disaster occurs. States that have been hit by hurricanes, tornadoes, floods, or earthquakes can apply for federal disaster aid. The states can use this money to help rebuild areas destroyed or damaged by natural disasters.

✓ **Check Your Understanding**

1. In which three areas do the states have general power to protect their people?

2. Describe at least one way in which a state can protect its people in each of the areas named in Question 1.

3. For what kinds of programs do states receive aid from the federal government?

Government Skills

FINDING STATE CAPITALS

A capital is the place where much of the work of government takes place. The capital of the United States is Washington, D.C. The federal government buildings are there. Government workers often have both homes and offices there.

Each state has a capital city, too. The state's legislative and executive branches conduct their work there. Do you know your state's capital? The map on the next two pages shows all 50 states and their capital cities. Each state capital is indicated with a ★. The nation's capital is indicated with ⊛.

Study the map. Then answer these questions.

1. What states surround Washington, D.C.?

2. What is the capital of the state where you live?

3. What states border your state? What are their capitals?

4. Which two states border no other states?

5. Which state capitals are located along the Mississippi River?

6. Which state capital is the most northern on the west coast of the United States?

7. Which state capital is the most northern on the east coast of the United States?

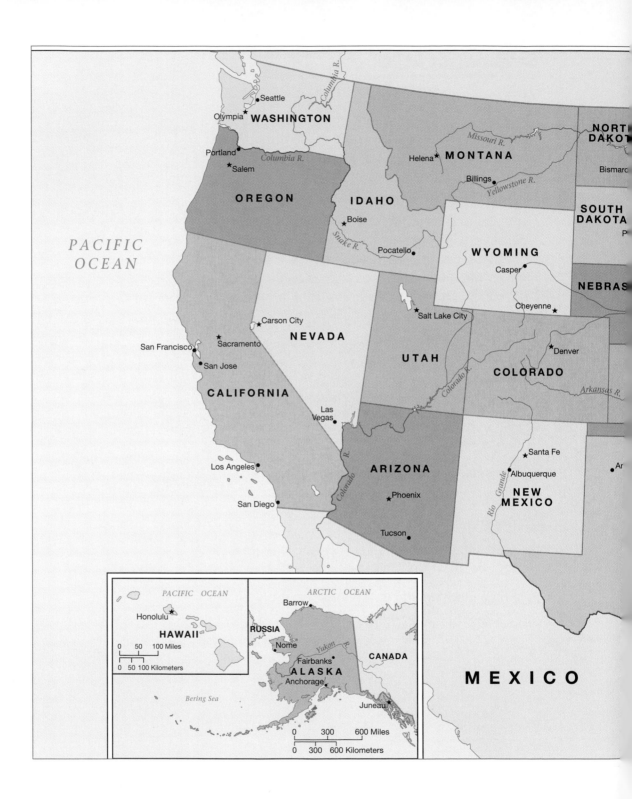

PACIFIC OCEAN

Seattle
Olympia ★
WASHINGTON

Columbia R.

NORTH DAKOTA

Portland
Salem ★

Columbia R.

Missouri R.

Helena ★ MONTANA

Billings
Yellowstone R.

Bismarck

OREGON

IDAHO

Boise

SOUTH DAKOTA

Snake R.

Pocatello

WYOMING

Casper

NEBRAS

PACIFIC
OCEAN

Carson City ★

NEVADA

Salt Lake City ★

Cheyenne ★

San Francisco
Sacramento ★

San Jose

UTAH

Colorado R.

Denver ★

COLORADO

Arkansas R.

CALIFORNIA

Las
Vegas

Colorado R.

Los Angeles

Santa Fe ★

Ar

ARIZONA

Albuquerque

San Diego

Phoenix ★

Rio Grande

NEW
MEXICO

Tucson

MEXICO

PACIFIC OCEAN

Honolulu ★

HAWAII

0   50   100 Miles

0 50 100 Kilometers

ARCTIC OCEAN

Barrow

RUSSIA

Nome

Fairbanks
Yukon

CANADA

ALASKA
Anchorage

Bering Sea

Juneau ★

0   300   600 Miles

0   300   600 Kilometers

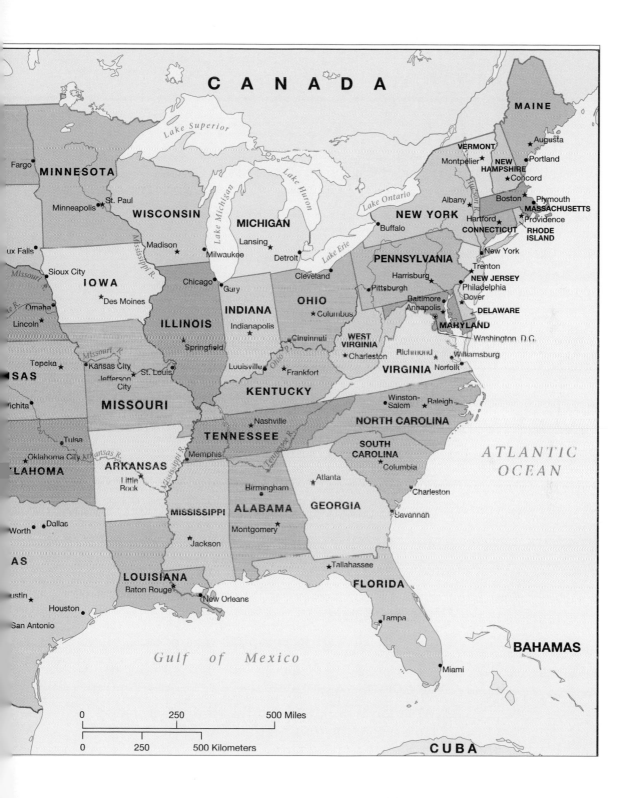

CANADA

Lake Superior

Lake Michigan

Lake Huron

Lake Ontario

Lake Erie

Fargo

MINNESOTA

Minneapolis • • St. Paul

WISCONSIN

Madison ★

Milwaukee •

MICHIGAN

Lansing ★

Detroit •

ux Falls

ix Falls

Sioux City •

Missouri

IOWA

Des Moines ★

Omaha •

Lincoln ★

Chicago •

• Gary

INDIANA

Indianapolis ★

OHIO

Cleveland •

Columbus ★

Cincinnati •

Ohio R.

MAINE

Augusta ★

VERMONT

Montpelier ★

NEW HAMPSHIRE

Concord ★

Portland •

Albany ★

NEW YORK

Buffalo •

Boston ★

Plymouth •

MASSACHUSETTS

Hartford ★

Providence ★

CONNECTICUT

RHODE ISLAND

PENNSYLVANIA

Harrisburg ★

Pittsburgh •

New York •

Trenton ★

NEW JERSEY

Philadelphia •

Dover ★

Baltimore •

Annapolis ★

DELAWARE

MARYLAND

Washington, D.C. •

WEST VIRGINIA

Charleston ★

Richmond ★

Williamsburg •

Norfolk •

VIRGINIA

Topeka ★

SAS

Kansas City •

Jefferson City ★

St. Louis •

MISSOURI

Springfield ★

Louisville •

Frankfort ★

KENTUCKY

Nashville •

TENNESSEE

Memphis •

Arkansas R.

Tennessee R.

Winston-Salem •

Raleigh ★

NORTH CAROLINA

ATLANTIC OCEAN

ichita •

Tulsa •

Oklahoma City ★

LAHOMA

ARKANSAS

Little Rock ★

Mississippi R.

MISSISSIPPI

Jackson ★

ALABAMA

Montgomery ★

Birmingham •

GEORGIA

Atlanta ★

SOUTH CAROLINA

Columbia ★

Charleston •

Savannah •

Worth

Dallas •

AS

ustin ★

Houston •

San Antonio

LOUISIANA

Baton Rouge ★

New Orleans •

Tallahassee ★

FLORIDA

Tampa •

Miami •

BAHAMAS

Gulf of Mexico

CUBA

| 0 | 250 | 500 Miles |

| 0 | 250 | 500 Kilometers |

Chapter
10 ▶ Review

Summary

The United States is a large and varied country. Every state has its own government.
The U.S. Constitution puts limits on the powers of the states. However, the Constitution also reserves certain powers for the states.
Each state has its own constitution. The state constitutions list the powers the states have within their own borders. They can pass laws, establish courts, borrow money, and set taxes.
Sometimes, the states work with the federal government to solve national problems.

federal aid

alliance

illegal

reserved

Vocabulary Review

Complete each sentence with a term from the list.

1. Money given to the states to solve problems is called _____.

2. If someone breaks the law, then that person has done something _____.

3. An _____ is a partnership of several nations.

4. When something is _____, it is being saved.

Chapter Quiz

Write your answers in complete sentences.

1. What two kinds of special laws may a state pass to take care of its own needs?

2. What kinds of powers did the 13 original states have before the Constitution was written?

3. What part of the Constitution spells out the powers denied to the states?

4. In what four basic ways are the state constitutions like the U.S. Constitution?

5. In what ways may a state protect the health, safety, and well-being of its people? List one way for each.

6. What happens to a state law that violates the U.S. Constitution?

7. **Critical Thinking** In what way would the 1962 laws requiring morning prayers in public schools in New York, Pennsylvania, and Maryland have conflicted with the First Amendment's guarantee of freedom of religion?

8. **Critical Thinking** Why does the federal government give federal aid to the states?

Write About Government

Complete the following activity.

Look at the statements below. Then decide whether a state has the power to take the action described in each statement. Write *Yes* or *No* next to each number. Then write a brief explanation telling why a state may or may not do such a thing.

1. A state puts a picture of its discoverer, Miles Patterson, on every $20 bill.

2. A state sets a speed limit of 55 miles per hour on all its highways.

Texas state legislators review bills during the opening session.

Learning Objectives

- Explain how state legislatures are organized and who their members are.

- Describe how state laws are made.

- Identify three ways the people of a state may take direct part in lawmaking and government.

Words to Know

assembly	a branch of the state legislature in some states
district	a part of a state that elects one state representative or state senator
initiative	the process by which the people of a state introduce and vote on proposed laws
petition	a written notice signed by many people that asks the government to take some action
referendum	the process by which the people of a state force their legislature to submit proposed bills for voter approval
recall	a way for the people to remove a state government official from office

The State Legislatures

The legislative branches of the states operate very much like the legislative branch of the federal government. Most state legislatures have two houses—a lower house and an upper house. The one exception is the state of Nebraska. It has a one-house legislature called the state senate.

The state legislatures hold sessions once a year. These sessions last three to four months. Like the U.S. Congress, the legislatures have committees that study bills to deal with different problems. The committees either kill the bills or send them to the full legislature for a vote.

Each house of the state legislature has a leader or presiding officer. In the lower house, the leader is the Speaker. In the upper house, it is usually a president *pro tempore.*

In each case, the leader appoints committees and committee chairpersons. In addition, the leader runs the sessions of the house and decides who gets to speak on proposed bills.

The Lower House A state's lower house is the larger of its legislative houses. It is usually called the house of representatives or the **assembly.** Its members are elected from **districts.** Each state is divided into districts that have equal populations. Each district elects one or more representatives. Alaska has 40 state representatives. Each one represents about 10,000 people. New Hampshire has 400 state representatives. Each represents about 2,300 people. You can see that districts differ from state to state.

Most state representatives serve two-year terms. Many representatives work only part-time for their state's government. Because state legislative sessions run only a few months, the representatives work at other jobs for the rest of the year. Like the U.S. House of Representatives, a state's lower house is called the "people's house." State representatives are often the legislators closest to the voters.

The Upper House The upper house in every state is called the state senate. The state senate always has fewer members than the lower house. The members usually serve four-year terms.

Members of the state senate are called state senators. They are elected from senate districts. Alaska has 20 state senators. Each represents about 20,000 people. Minnesota has 67 state senators. Each represents about 60,000 people. Like state representatives, state senators work only part-time for their state's government.

Remember
Members of the U.S. House of Representatives serve two-year terms.

✓ Check Your Understanding

1. Name at least two similarities between the state legislative branches and the federal legislative branch.

2. Why do many state legislators have other jobs for part of the year?

Passing State Laws

The state legislatures are run like the U.S. Congress in more ways than organization and leadership. They make laws the same way Congress does. They follow the same steps.

1. A state representative or senator writes a bill.

2. The bill is studied, debated, and passed by a committee in the house where it began.

3. The bill is debated and passed by a majority of members in the house where it began.

4. The bill goes to the other house, where it is studied by a committee.

5. The bill is debated and passed by a majority of the second house.

6. A special committee works out any differences in the bills passed by the two houses. Then the bill is passed again by both houses.

7. The state's chief executive can sign the bill into law or veto it. If vetoed, the bill must be passed in each house by a two-thirds majority to become law.

The People's Power

How much power do a state's people really have over the laws that get passed? Of course, the people elect their state representatives and senators. They try to vote for men and women who will pass laws that will benefit the public. However, the people have even more powers in state government. In many states, there are three ways that the people can take *direct* action.

Initiative About half the states allow **initiatives** in the making of new laws. Suppose the people of a state want a new, tougher law against drunk drivers. People who want the law write a proposal for it. Then they try to get other people to sign this initiative **petition.** They have to collect thousands of signatures from people who support the law. If enough people sign, the initiative is then voted on in the next statewide election. If the voters approve it, it becomes law. If not, it dies.

Referendum About half the states allow **referendums.** Referendums force a state legislature to let the voters decide on a bill the legislature is considering. Suppose the people of a state want to stop a bill that raises taxes from becoming law. People who want to stop the bill sign their names to a referendum petition. If enough people sign it, the bill is taken away from the legislature. Instead, the people themselves get the chance to vote on it in the next statewide election. If a majority votes for the referendum, the bill is stopped from becoming a law. A referendum can even be called on a bill that has already been passed, as long as it has not yet gone into effect.

Recall About one-fourth of the states allow **recalls** by the people. In a recall, the people remove an elected state official from office before his or her term is finished. For example, suppose many people think that a state senator is doing a poor job. People who want the senator taken out of office sign a petition.

If enough people sign, a new election for the senator's job is held. The election is held right away, and anyone who wishes can run against the senator. Whoever gets the most votes wins the senate seat.

Citizenship and You

KNOWING YOUR STATE LAWMAKERS

Ask your teacher or librarian to help you find the answers to the following questions. You may find the answers on the Internet.

1. What are the name, two addresses, and phone numbers of your state senator? (One address is at the state capital. The other address is near where you live.)

2. What are the name, two addresses, and phone numbers of your state representative?

3. **a.** How many state senators are in your state's legislature?
   b. How many people does each senator represent?

4. **a.** How many representatives are in your state's lower house?
   b. How many people are in each house district?

5. Write a letter to one of these state lawmakers. It might look like this:

[today's date]
Senator (or Representative) _____
[address]
[city, state, zip code]
Dear Senator (or Representative) _____:
    I am a student trying to learn more about government. Please tell me what committees you are on. What laws have you helped to write or pass? Which laws or ideas are you against?
    What is your "other" job—the one you have when the state legislature is not meeting? Thank you for taking the time to answer my questions.
Sincerely,
[Sign your name.]
[Print or type your name and address clearly.]

You may be able to send your letter by e-mail.

LANDMARK CHANGES IN THE LAW
California's Voter Revolt

Sometimes voters use initiatives when the legislature refuses to listen to their wishes. This has happened in California more than once. In 1978, the price of land and homes was rising fast. California voters were angry about rising property taxes. An initiative passed that cut property taxes to 1 percent of the value of the property. That saved each homeowner hundreds of dollars a year. Voters in other states soon followed California's lead. This forced local governments to "tighten their belts" and cut back on spending.

In 1988, California voters again became angry. This time, they were reacting to the high cost of insurance, especially car insurance. For years, people had asked California legislators for laws to lower the cost of insurance. However, for various reasons, the legislators refused to act.

Leaders of the California group Voter Revolt celebrated the passage of their initiative to cut state insurance rates.

Finally, certain voters got tired of being ignored. They formed a group called Voter Revolt to Cut Insurance Rates. Hundreds of thousands of people signed an initiative to cut California insurance rates by 20 percent. Insurance companies and their supporters were strongly against the idea. They claimed any cut in rates would cause them to lose a lot of money. Some companies even claimed they would be forced to go out of business. The insurance companies spent more than $70 million to fight the insurance rate cuts. The Voter Revolt group had only $2 million to pay for its campaign.

The insurance companies also came up with their own initiative. This plan called for lower rates and quick payments on insurance claims. That part of their plan sounded good enough. However, their initiative also cut back on the amount of money a person could ask for in a claim. People could actually end up with less insurance. Furthermore, if the initiative passed, it would cancel the Voter Revolt initiative.

The question became the most argued issue in the 1988 California elections. The newspapers, television, and radio covered the contest heavily. This helped the Voter Revolt group. The more people who knew about the Voter Revolt initiative, the more votes it was likely to gain.

When the results came in, California voters had joined against the insurance companies. The voters passed the Voter Revolt initiative to cut insurance rates. Within a few weeks, lawmakers and voter groups from 30 other states showed interest in passing similar laws. Once again, the people of California had sent a *direct action* message to their legislature.

You Decide

Are you for or against a law cutting back insurance rates in your state? What are your reasons?

Summary

The state legislative branches are organized very much like the federal legislative branch. Each state except Nebraska has a two-house legislature.

A state's lower house is the larger of the legislative houses. It is usually called the house of representatives, or the assembly. A state's upper house is called the state senate. It has fewer members than the lower house.

Initiatives, referendums, and recalls allow the people to take direct action in lawmaking and government.

Vocabulary Review

Write *true* or *false*. If the statement is false, change the underlined term to make it true.

1. A <u>petition</u> is the method by which citizens force the legislature to submit bills for voter approval.

2. In some states, an <u>assembly</u> is part of the state legislature.

3. There is one state senator and one state representative elected from each <u>district</u>.

4. A <u>law</u> is a written notice requesting the government to respond to a situation.

5. People can <u>recall</u> a state government official if they are not satisfied with the official's performance.

Chapter Quiz

Write your answers in complete sentences.

1. In what three ways do the state legislative branches resemble the federal government's legislative branch?

2. What does the leader of each state legislature do?

3. What is the difference between an initiative and a referendum?

4. What is a recall?

5. What role does the petition play in direct government action by the people?

6. **Critical Thinking** Why are there so many similarities between state governments and the federal government?

7. **Critical Thinking** When do you think a problem should be handled through a voter referendum?

Write About Government

Complete the following activity. Work with a classmate.

1. What is the name of your state legislature's lower house? What is the name of its upper house?

2. Name two ways that your state legislature is like the U.S. Congress. Name two ways that your legislature is different from the U.S. Congress.

3. During what part of the year does your state legislature meet? For how many months?

4. Describe one piece of legislation recently passed by your state legislature.

Governor Jeanne Shaheen, New Hampshire's first woman governor, signs a bill as Martin Luther King III looks on. The bill honors his father, Dr. Martin Luther King, Jr., by including his birthday as a state holiday.

Learning Objectives

- Explain the roles and powers of state governors.
- Explain the roles and duties of other elected members of the state's executive branch.
- Identify four state executive branch departments.
- Describe how the jobs of governor and U.S. President are similar and different.

Words to Know

governor	the leader of the executive branch of state government
lieutenant governor	the person next in line for the job of governor; takes office if the governor dies, resigns, or is unable to carry out the job
secretary of state	the person in state government who keeps state records and runs state elections
superintendent of public instruction	in some states, the person who runs the state public schools

The State Governor

The **governor** is the most important person in state government. The governor stands for state government and all the things it does.

Every state has its own laws about who can be governor. However, all states have certain similar qualifications for the office. The governor must be a U.S. citizen and have lived in the state for some time—five years in most states. The governor must also be a certain age to run for office—30 years old in most states.

Most governors serve four-year terms. The idea is that a governor needs four years to carry out his or her plans for the job. However, in New Hampshire and Vermont, a governor serves only two years. These states think short terms keep the governor in closer touch with the needs of the people. If the people are unhappy with the governor, they can elect a new one in just two years.

The Jobs of the Governor

A state is much like a country within a country. Furthermore, running a state government is much like running the federal government. The governor is head of the state executive branch. This means a governor has many of the same jobs as the President of the United States.

Chief Executive The governor has the power to carry out state laws. The governor also draws up the state budget. The budget must also be passed by the legislature. The lawmakers may want to change some parts of the budget. The governor must work with the lawmakers.

Chief of State The governor makes speeches, greets visitors, and appears at special important gatherings.

Chief Diplomat The governor often meets with other state governors, officials of the federal government, and foreign representatives.

Chief Lawmaker The governor does not have the power to make laws directly. That is always the job of the legislative branch. The governor can veto bills and the governor can propose new laws. These laws usually have a good chance of being passed.

Commander-in-Chief The governor is commander-in-chief of the state's National Guard. The governor has the power to call out the Guard in any emergency, from natural disasters to riots.

Party Chief The governor is the state leader of his or her political party. Usually, the governor works closely with other members of the party. In addition, the governor may also help the party members get elected to other state offices.

Washington Governor Gary Locke (right) greets Nelson Mandela, former president of South Africa, during a visit to Seattle.

As you can see, the governor's job is like the job of the President in many ways. However, the President does not have to share executive powers with others. State governors must share their powers with others who are elected as part of the state's executive branch.

Other Elected State Officers

The following people are elected to help carry out state laws. They usually work as a team with the governor. However, they answer to the people, not to the governor.

Lieutenant Governor In 42 states, the second most important official is the **lieutenant governor**. This official becomes governor if the governor is unable to carry out the job. In many states, the lieutenant governor presides over the state senate.

Attorney General Every state has an attorney general. The attorney general is the state's chief lawyer. The attorney general advises the governor, the legislature, and other state officials on matters of the law.

Secretary of State Every state has a **secretary of state**. The secretary of state is elected to keep official state records. The secretary of state runs all statewide elections and makes sure the elections are fair.

Superintendent of Public Instruction The **superintendent of public instruction** is the chief education official in the state. The superintendent works with the board of education. Together they enforce the state's requirements for learning and teaching.

State Departments

A state has many other executive departments besides the education, state, and attorney general's offices. State governments must meet the needs of all their people. The states have departments in areas such as health, transportation, parks, and prisons. The heads of these departments make up the rest of the governor's team. The governor chooses the people who will help enforce his or her policies within their departments.

The governor decides how much money each department gets to spend every year. The departments can do only those things the governor has put into the budget. Suppose the transportation department decides to build a new bridge. The money in the budget has been marked for road repairs. In that case, the bridge must wait. The money must be used to fix the roads. Much of the money for the budget comes from taxes paid by the people of the state.

States also operate special boards that give tests to certain professionals and workers in the trades. Doctors and lawyers are some of those who must pass tests to obtain licenses to work in the state. Others are teachers, builders, and plumbers.

✓ **Check Your Understanding**

1. Name three requirements all governors must meet to hold office.

2. Name two roles governors have. Briefly describe each role.

3. Name one other elected official of a state's executive branch besides the governor. Describe that official's duty.

The Governor and the President

Some people think that the job of governor is good training for the job of President. In many ways, the two jobs *are* alike. However, they are different in three important ways.

First, a governor's power is limited to just one state. The governor of California has no say about what happens in Texas. The President has power over all states. Second, the governor has no power over the U.S. armed forces. The governor is only commander-in-chief of his or her state's National Guard. States may not form armies. Third, the governor must share power with other elected officials of the state's executive branch. The President does not have to share executive power.

Even with these differences, the governor's job is very much like that of the President. Both the governor and the President are leaders of the

Between 1900
and 1992, seven
governors became
President: Theodore
Roosevelt, Woodrow
Wilson, Calvin
Coolidge, Franklin D.
Roosevelt, Jimmy
Carter, Ronald
Reagan, and Bill
Clinton.

executive branches of government. Both get to live
in government-owned houses. Both have several
jobs: chief executive, chief diplomat, chief lawmaker,
commander-in-chief, and party chief. The governor
chooses some heads of executive departments. The
President chooses the heads of all federal executive
departments. Both the governor and the President
draw up budgets. Both have the veto power. Both
also have the important job of following the will of
the people.

It is not surprising that several governors have gone
on to become Presidents. Of 42 Presidents, 16 were
once governors. This shows that the job of running a
state may often lead to the job of running a country.

*The nation's governors often meet to discuss various problems the states
have in common.*

GOVERNMENT ISSUES
The Governor of Texas Against the Texas Legislature

Sam Houston was elected governor of Texas in 1859. As a hero of the war for Texas' independence from Mexico, he was the most popular person in the state. Just two years later, he found himself at "war" with his own legislature—and out of a job.

In the spring of 1861, several southern states voted to leave the Union of the United States. The southern states were determined to keep slavery. The new President, Abraham Lincoln, was very much against slavery.

Texas had become a state in 1845. Sam Houston had worked hard to bring Texas into the Union. Now in 1861, most of the people of Texas wanted to join the South. Those in the legislature wanted to join the South, too. Sam Houston was firmly against the idea. He said that Texas had joined the Union, not just the North or the South.

Houston traveled all over the state. He tried to convince people that Texas should remain in the Union. No one wanted to hear him. They threw rocks, yelled, and hissed at him. In one town, a gunpowder keg was blown up just outside his bedroom.

Finally, the Texas legislature called a special meeting to withdraw from the Union. Houston refused to take part in it. The legislature voted 109 to 2 to join the South. Every state officer was called to swear to be true to the new Confederacy of southern states. Sam Houston refused. Because of his refusal, Houston was removed from office.

Sam Houston had made a choice. He had chosen the interests of the nation he loved over the popular wishes of his state. It was the most difficult choice a governor ever had to make.

You Decide

Did Sam Houston make the right choice by refusing to lead Texas out of the Union? Give reasons for your answer.

Summary

The governor heads the executive branch of state government. The governor has six major roles: chief executive, chief of state, chief diplomat, chief lawmaker, commander-in-chief, and party chief.

The governor must share executive power with other elected officials. Four of the most important state officials are: the lieutenant governor, the attorney general, the secretary of state, and the superintendent of public instruction.

State governments must meet the many needs of all their people. Some state departments that meet these needs are: health, transportation, parks, and prisons. The governor chooses the heads of these departments.

States also operate special boards that give tests to certain professionals and other workers. They must pass the tests to obtain licenses to work.

secretary of state
lieutenant governor
governor
superintendent of public instruction

Vocabulary Review

Write the term from the list that matches the definition below.

1. The official that runs state elections

2. The leader of the state executive branch

3. The official that would take over if the governor resigns

4. The person who runs state public schools

Chapter Quiz

Complete numbers 1–7 by filling in the correct word or phrase. Then answer questions 8 and 9 in complete sentences.

1. Most state governors are elected to terms of _____ years.

2. When a governor meets with other government officials, he or she is acting as _____.

3. When a governor proposes a new law, he or she is acting as _____.

4. When a governor calls up the state's National Guard, he or she is acting as _____.

5. Two elected state officials with whom the governor shares power are _____ and _____.

6. The chief education official in the state is called the _____.

7. The governor decides how the state will spend its money by preparing a _____.

8. **Critical Thinking** Why do doctors and lawyers have to pass state tests and obtain licenses?

9. **Critical Thinking** Why do states spend more money on education than on any other part of government?

Write About Government

Complete the following activity.

Copy each sentence below. Decide whether it describes the job of *governor*, *President*, or *both*. Then write the word that correctly applies.

1. In some states, this person may be elected for two years.

2. This person serves as chief of state by making speeches and greeting visitors.

3. This person is commander-in-chief of the U.S. armed forces.

4. This person can veto bills passed by the legislative branch.

Chapter 13 State Courts

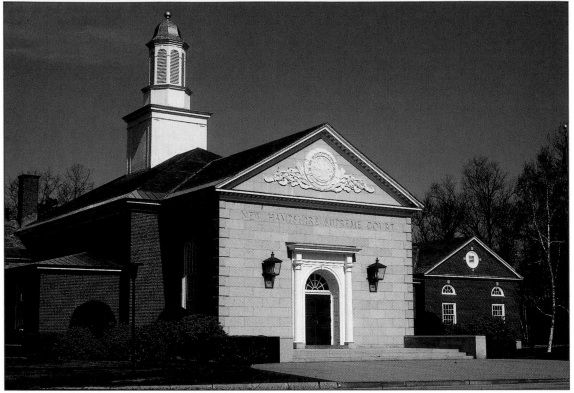

This is the New Hampshire State Supreme Court building in Concord.

Learning Objectives

- Identify the kinds of cases heard in the state courts.
- Explain the roles of judges and juries in state trial courts.
- Explain the role and responsibilities of the state courts of appeals.
- Define the role and responsibilities of the state supreme court.

Words to Know

assault	an attack on a person by one or more other persons
intoxicated	drunk
divorce	civil court case to end a marriage
witness	a person who knows or has seen or heard things that are important to a case and is called upon to tell these things in court
deadlocked	a situation in which a jury in a trial cannot reach a decision

The State Court System

The judicial branch of state government operates very much like the judicial branch of the federal government. The state courts have the responsibility to explain the laws and the power to punish those who violate them. As with the federal system, state courts hear civil cases and criminal cases separately.

The state courts handle cases that deal only with state laws. They hear three main kinds of cases.

1. Cases dealing with the state constitution Suppose a state passes a law that says the police can search 500 cars a day for illegal drugs. However, the state's constitution guarantees that no person can be searched without a special paper signed by a judge. This law can be reviewed in the state courts.

2. Criminal cases dealing with state laws Cases that involve such crimes as robbery, **assault**, and driving while **intoxicated** are tried in state court.

3. **Civil cases within one state** Civil cases have to do with broken promises or a disagreement about money. **Divorce** cases are also civil cases. Other civil cases have to do with the harm caused by accidents or from using poorly made goods.

State Trial Courts: Judges and Juries

Remember
The federal judicial system is made up of district courts, courts of appeals, and the Supreme Court.

Most states have three kinds of courts. (See chart on page 171.) The lowest state courts are state trial courts. Most state cases begin here.

Every state is divided into judicial districts. Each district has its own trial court. Ohio has 88 state trial courts. However, Rhode Island, a much smaller state, has only four.

Each trial court has one judge and a jury. The judge makes sure that the trial is fair and that it follows the rules of law. The judge decides what facts can be presented. The judge may decide that certain kinds of questions cannot be asked. In addition, the judge usually decides the sentence if someone is found guilty by the jury in a criminal trial.

Generally, the people on the jury live in the judicial district. A new jury is picked for each case. Twelve people normally serve on a jury. For some civil cases, smaller juries are chosen.

During the trial, all the facts of a case are presented. The jury listens to **witnesses** and lawyers for both sides. In criminal cases, the jury decides whether the person on trial is guilty or innocent. In civil cases, the jury decides who is right and who is wrong. Often, it decides how the wrong must be repaid. Usually, the payment is made in money.

In most cases, *all* the people on the jury must agree. If they cannot, another trial is held, and another jury hears the case.

✓ Check Your Understanding

1. Name three kinds of cases handled by state courts.

2. Name one example of a criminal case. Name one example of a civil case.

Focus on Government

THE JURY SYSTEM

Why do the courts need twelve people to help decide cases? Why not allow the judge—or the lawyers—to decide whether the person is innocent or guilty?

Think about how much a person loses if he or she is found guilty. A guilty person loses freedom, loses money, and loses his or her good name. One person might make a mistake. Twelve people representing many backgrounds and opinions are less likely to make a mistake.

Often, it takes days or even weeks for a jury to make its decision. Sometimes, a case leaves many questions in the minds of the people on the jury. If all twelve people cannot agree, the jury is **deadlocked.** Usually, a new trial with a new jury will be ordered. Sometimes, the case against the accused will be dropped.

State Courts of Appeals: Reviewing Trials

The next highest courts in the state system are the state courts of appeals. Sometimes, a person who is found guilty in a trial court believes that the trial was unfair. That person can ask a higher court to review the case. Such a case usually goes to the state court of appeals. All the states have one or more such courts.

The state court of appeals has a judge but no jury. No new trial is held. The judge decides only whether the lower court's trial was fair and followed the law. The judge looks for mistakes that might have been made. If mistakes are found, the judge can order a new trial.

The State Supreme Court

In most states, the highest state court is the state supreme court. This court reviews cases from both lower courts. It also has the final word on the meaning of the state constitution and state laws. Sometimes, a state supreme court case is reviewed by the U.S. Supreme Court. This happens only when there is a question raised about federal laws or the U.S. Constitution.

A state's supreme court is made up of several judges called justices. Together, they decide the questions brought before the state's highest court.

Most cases never reach the state supreme court. Thousands of cases are handled each year by lower courts. Very few are ever appealed to the supreme court. Even then, this court can decide not to take a case. There must be a very important question at the heart of the case.

Most state supreme courts review at least 100 cases a year. The cases concern the meanings of the state's laws or constitution. Most of them are cases on appeal from lower courts.

Cases appealed to the state supreme court are handled like cases appealed to other courts. No new trial is held. The court goes over the case records. It decides whether the trial was fair. It checks to see that all the laws and rules of court were followed. The justices can decide to uphold the rulings of the lower court or order a new trial. Usually, this is the final appeal that can be made of a state court case.

The chart below shows how both the federal and the state courts are set up.

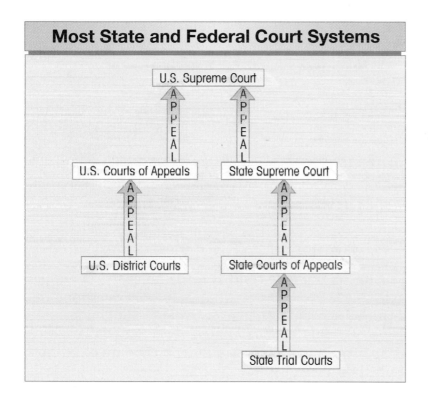

Most State and Federal Court Systems

U.S. Supreme Court

APPEAL

U.S. Courts of Appeals | State Supreme Court

APPEAL

U.S. District Courts | State Courts of Appeals

APPEAL

State Trial Courts

✓ **Check Your Understanding**

1. Where do most federal cases begin?

2. Where do most state cases begin?

3. How many people usually serve on a jury?

LANDMARK CHANGES IN THE LAW
The Case of Clarence Gideon

Clarence Gideon's trial began on August 4, 1961, in a Florida trial court. Gideon was accused of robbing a local poolroom in the early morning hours of June 3. On the first day of the trial, the judge asked Gideon whether he was ready. Gideon said no. He did not have a lawyer because he did not have any money. He asked the court for a free lawyer. Florida laws allowed the courts to give people free legal help in some criminal cases. However, the laws did not allow for help in a case such as Gideon's. The judge decided there was no special reason to give Gideon a lawyer.

Gideon had to act as his own lawyer. The judge tried to help during the trial. Even with the judge's help, the jury found Gideon guilty. One witness said he had seen Gideon come out of the poolroom at 5:30 A.M. with a bottle of wine. The jury believed the witness. Gideon was sentenced to five years in jail.

Gideon wrote to the U.S. Supreme Court. He asked to have the state court's decision overturned. He believed that being put on trial without a lawyer was against the U.S. Constitution. The Supreme Court decided to hear the case.

Gideon himself did not appear before the Supreme Court. Instead, the Court appointed a well-known lawyer named Abe Fortas to represent him. Fortas pointed out to the Court that the Constitution promises everyone a fair trial. Gideon did not get a fair trial, he said, because he could not have a lawyer. Because of this, argued Fortas, Florida's law went against the U.S. Constitution.

The Supreme Court agreed with Fortas in *Gideon* v. *Wainwright*. It ordered Florida to give Gideon a new trial and a lawyer to represent him.

When Gideon went back to court, this time, he had a lawyer. The main witness was back, telling how he had seen Gideon coming out of the poolroom at 5:30 A.M. Gideon's lawyer questioned this witness closely. He showed how the witness's story might not be true. The jury now could not say for sure that Gideon had robbed the poolroom. It decided he was not guilty.

Because of Clarence Gideon's appeal, he received a new trial and was found innocent. However, Gideon's case had much more far-reaching effects than just for himself. Because of his case, all states have to provide a free lawyer to anyone who cannot pay for one.

You Decide

Should all states have to provide free lawyers to people accused of crimes? Why or why not?

Abe Fortas was the lawyer appointed by the Supreme Court to represent Clarence Gideon.

Summary

State courts hear three main kinds of cases: (1) cases dealing with the state constitution; (2) criminal cases dealing with state laws; and (3) civil cases within the state.

The lowest state courts are the trial courts. Every state is divided into judicial districts. Each district has its own trial court. Each trial court has one judge and a jury.

The people on the jury generally live in judicial districts. A new jury is chosen for each case. Twelve people usually serve on a jury.

The next highest courts are the state courts of appeals. These courts review cases from the trial courts.

The highest state court in most states is the state supreme court. The state's highest court has the final word on the meaning of the state constitution and state laws.

deadlocked

assault

intoxicated

witness

divorce

Vocabulary Review

Complete each sentence with a term from the list.

1. A person who is _____ has had too much alcohol to drink.

2. When a jury cannot make a verdict it is _____.

3. A _____ is called to give testimony during trials.

4. A _____ is a civil court case.

5. When someone commits _____, he or she harms another person.

Chapter Quiz

Write your answers in complete sentences.

1. What are two similarities between the state court and the federal court systems?

2. What are two examples of criminal cases handled by state courts?

3. What are two examples of civil cases handled by state courts?

4. What are judicial districts?

5. What is the role of a judge in the state trial courts?

6. What is the role of a witness in the state trial courts?

7. What happens when a jury is deadlocked?

8. Where are cases from the state trial courts appealed first?

9. **Critical Thinking** What do you think is the most important responsibility of the state court of appeals? Explain your reasons.

10. **Critical Thinking** What can happen when the U.S. Supreme Court reviews a case decided by a state supreme court?

Write About Government

Complete the following activity.

Look through your city's newspaper and find a story about a trial being held in state court. Then answer the following questions.

1. Describe the kind of civil or criminal case being heard.

2. What was the name of the person on trial?

3. What was the name of the trial judge?

4. Was there an outcome to the trial? What was it?

Chapter 14

Local Government

San Francisco Mayor Willie Brown speaks before a crowd at a mayors' conference.

Learning Objectives

- Explain the organization and functions of local governments.
- Identify key officials of county governments, and describe their responsibilities.
- Identify and describe the three main types of city government plans.
- Identify local government departments, and describe their responsibilities.
- Identify and describe the various community services that local governments provide.

Words to Know

local	close to home, nearby; having to do with a city, county, town, village, or other small government
county board	small group of people elected to make laws for and run the government of the county
assessor	a local official who decides how much tax people must pay on their land, houses, buildings, and other things they own
district attorney	a lawyer who works for the government and brings accused persons to trial
prosecute	to take legal action against someone in court
city council	small group of people elected to make laws and run a city's government
mayor	a person elected as chief executive of a city
city manager	a person who works for a city government as the top administrator
city commission	small group of people elected to make laws for a city and run city government; each person on it is also the head of a local department
community services office	office that helps people find out what services they can get from county, city, or town government
community group	a group run by private organizations to help people in need

What Local Government Does

Are the streets in your town safe to drive on? Is there a hospital nearby if you need one? Are there police officers and firefighters you can call if you are in trouble? Your **local** government handles these things and many more. A local government will never stop a war between countries. It will not send people to the moon or build a 500-mile highway. Instead, it takes care of things close to home.

Local governments are found in villages, towns, cities, and counties. The United States has more than 19,000 cities. Some are huge and have large governments. Some are small and have small governments. A town in the desert of New Mexico has different problems than a town in the rainy mountains of Washington. Each town has a government that meets its local needs.

In some ways, local governments are like state and federal governments. Cities and counties have their own written laws. They have leaders elected by the people. They have three branches of government—legislative, executive, and judicial. However, local governments are different in one important way. In most cities and counties, the executive and legislative jobs are done by one group of leaders. The ones who make the laws are also responsible for seeing they are carried out.

County Government

A state is divided into land areas called counties. County governments are really arms of the state government. County governments carry out the laws of the state in local places.

The work of running a county takes place in a town or city called the county seat. There, the **county board** meets to find ways to solve any problems in the county. Between five and nine people are elected to the county board. Its job is to make county laws and to carry them out. The board has the power to set taxes and decide how the money should be spent. It works with the people in many county departments.

Remember
Review Chapter 4 to be sure what each branch of government does.

The county might have a parks department, a health department, and a sheriff's department, among others.

Other elected officials help the county board. One of these officials is the county sheriff. The sheriff makes sure that people follow the laws of the county. Another is the county **assessor**. The assessor decides how much tax people will pay on land, buildings, or other property they own. The **district attorney** represents the county in court cases. The district attorney **prosecutes** people who have violated state or county laws. The county clerk keeps track of all births, deaths, and marriages in the county.

Government Fact

Two states do not have counties. Alaska has *districts*. Louisiana has *parishes*.

Marriage licenses are issued at the county clerk's office.

City Government

Different cities set up their governments in different ways. They usually follow one of these three plans.

1. **City council–mayor plan** In most cities, the citizens elect a **city council.** Five to nine people are elected to the council. Each one represents a section of the city. Another person is elected **mayor.** The mayor leads the city council meetings and is the chief executive of the city.

   Some cities give the mayor strong powers to carry out laws. Others keep the mayor fairly weak in executive power. In some cities, the council keeps both the legislative and executive power. In those cities, the council passes laws, makes the city budget, and hires and fires city workers. The mayor may have a few special jobs, such as leading the council meetings. However, the mayor is not much more than just another person on the council. This is known as the "weak mayor plan."

   In other cities, the mayor is a real chief executive. These mayors can veto laws passed by the council. They hire and fire city workers, and they make up the city budget. This is known as the "strong mayor plan."

   Mayors also serve in ceremonial roles. They cut ribbons at the openings of new buildings or bridges. They speak before crowds at the openings of town festivals. The mayor also represents the city or town to other cities.

2. **City council–city manager plan** This kind of city government also has a city council. Sometimes, it has a mayor. However, under this plan, a **city manager** is hired by the council to carry out the executive jobs. City managers have special training

You Decide

Why may a city council choose a "weak mayor plan" over a "strong mayor plan"?

to run a city just like a business. The manager appoints the heads of departments who are directly responsible to him or her.

3. **Commission plan** A **city commission** is made up of members, or commissioners, elected by the people of the city. Commissioners have the same power as city council members. Usually, each commissioner is also the head of a city department, such as the fire and police, health care, or recreation. Small towns and cities often use this plan of local government.

Government Fact

The city hall or town hall near where you live is where the city government makes laws and runs the government.

✓ **Check Your Understanding**

1. Name three things that local governments do.

2. How are local governments like the state and federal governments?

Local Departments

Almost every local government has a *police* or *sheriff's department* and a *fire department*. Together, these departments protect the safety of the people in the city or county.

A *health department* may run local hospitals. It makes sure that state and county health laws are followed. Each restaurant has to meet the rules set by the local health department. All food, cooking, and serving areas must be clean and safe.

Many counties have a *street* or *road department*. This department maintains streets and street lights. In addition, it keeps roads and roadways in good working order.

Firefighters are on duty 24 hours a day to protect lives and property.

A *parks department* runs the local public parks and playgrounds. It may also run public beaches, swimming pools, lakes, and other kinds of recreational areas.

Local Government Services

These local departments can take care of most of the needs of a city or county's people. However, who takes care of the special needs and problems that small groups of people may have? What about the people who are sick and cannot pay for a doctor? What about older people who have no family or friends and no place to go? Local governments help them, too.

Most local governments have a **community services office** that can help these people. The workers are trained to answer people's questions. They know what the government can do to help. Here are some services many local governments pay for.

- **Low-cost health care** Most counties have a public health center where people can get health care for free or at low cost.

- **Help for senior citizens** Special local centers are set up for senior citizens to socialize and take part in activities. Many low-cost services may be offered to them. In most cities, senior citizens can use public transportation and receive meals at low cost.

- **Schooling for adults** Many local schools have night classes for adults who did not finish high school. Sometimes, there are classes for people who do not speak or read English well. Some of the money for these schools may come from state government.

These adults take an English class in the evening.

Community Groups

There are many other services that local governments provide for people. Even so, no government can meet all local needs. Most towns have many private **community groups** to help people in need. You probably have heard of the American Red Cross and the Salvation Army. These national organizations have offices in almost every city or county in the country. There are school groups, church groups, and many more groups that work together to help themselves and others. These groups help make each community a better place to live.

✓ **Check Your Understanding**

1. Name one form of city government. Briefly describe how it works.

2. Name two local government departments. Briefly describe their responsibilities.

Citizenship and You

LEARNING ABOUT YOUR LOCAL GOVERNMENT

You can find out about your local government in various ways. One way would be to look in your local newspaper. Another way would be to look in your local phone book under City or County Government. You could also research using the Internet.

Number a sheet of paper from 1 to 10. Then write the answers to the following questions. If you need help and are not sure where to look for an answer, ask your teacher or librarian.

1. What is the name of your town or city?

2. What is the name of your county?

3. In what city of your county is the county seat?

4. What is the name of the group that runs your county's government? Where does this group meet?

5. Name two of your county representatives.

6. **a.** Which plan of city government does your city use?
   b. What is the name of the group who runs your city government?
   c. Where does this group meet?

7. If your city has a mayor, what is his or her name?

8. **a.** List the names of three county departments that you have seen, visited, or received help from. Look them up in the County Government pages in your phone book.
   b. List three county departments that you did not know of before.

9. **a.** List the names of three city or town departments that you have heard of before. Look them up in the City Government pages in your phone book.
   b. List the names of three other departments that you have not heard of before.

10. Read a newspaper for two or three days in a row. Find as many stories as you can about your city and county governments. List four departments that you find in the newspaper.

Summary

Counties, cities, towns, and places close to home are run by local governments. County governments are the arms of state governments. The county governments carry out state laws in local places.

City government organization usually follows one of these plans: (1) city council–mayor plan; (2) city council–city manager plan; (3) commission plan.

Local governments have many departments that provide services for their citizens. Among these departments are: police, fire, health, street, and parks. Local governments also provide services for the special needs of some citizens. Most communities also have private groups to assist needy people.

Vocabulary Review

Write *true* or *false*. If the statement is false, change the underlined term to make it true.

1. A <u>city manager</u> brings people charged with a crime to trial.

2. The <u>mayor</u> is the chief executive of the city.

3. The <u>county board</u> is in charge of assessing people's property.

4. An organization to help the homeless is an example of a <u>city council</u>.

5. If a family wants to find out what services are provided in its city, it would ask the <u>community services office</u>.

Chapter Quiz

Write your answers in complete sentences.

1. What is the location of the county government called?

2. What is the name of the governing body in a county government?

3. What are the titles of two elected county officials? Describe their duties and responsibilities.

4. What is the difference between the city council-mayor plan and the city council-city manager plan of government?

5. What is the major difference between a city council and a city commission?

6. What are some of the services that local governments pay for?

7. Critical Thinking Why is there a local office to help people with special needs?

8. Critical Thinking Why are private community groups necessary?

Write About Government

Complete the following activity.

Think about the kind of government your town or city has. Then answer the following questions.

1. Do you think the government system in your town or city is a good one? Why or why not?

2. Are there any groups in your school that assist citizens in your community? Describe two of them.

Chapter 15 ▶ Making Local Laws

Petitions being signed in Denver, Colorado, called for an initiative that would allow voters to decide how growth will occur in their communities.

Learning Objectives

- Explain why communities have local laws.
- Identify the kinds of local laws communities have.
- Explain how local laws are made.
- Describe the ways citizens can take part in local governments.

Words to Know

property	the things that someone owns, such as land or buildings
disturbing the peace	to create trouble in a community or neighborhood
trespass	to enter or go onto a person's property without permission
vandalism	the destruction of a person's property

Why We Have Local Laws

In a town in Georgia, it is against the law for a chicken to cross any road inside the town limits. In a city in Indiana, it is against the law to carry a watermelon into a public park.

It is hard to know just why strange laws like these were passed. Somehow, the chickens or watermelons were keeping some people in those places from enjoying their rights. Local laws are usually made to protect the rights of citizens. Your town or county surely has some laws that are special just to where you live. You might be able to find some laws in your own city that are just as strange as the chicken law.

Laws often tell people what they cannot do, not what they can do. These local laws seem to limit people's rights. These limits protect the more important rights of all people. A building law may limit someone's right to put up any kind of building that person wants. However, such laws protect everyone from unsafe or poorly made buildings. A noise law might take away someone's right to have loud parties late at night. Yet, it protects the rights of the neighbors to get a good night's sleep.

Kinds of Local Laws

Some local laws are more important than others. Almost all of them are made either to protect people or to protect **property**.

Some laws protect people from being hurt. Others outlaw the keeping of lions, alligators, or other dangerous animals on personal property. Some laws set speed limits and control traffic to cut down car accidents. Still other laws tell how many people a room or an elevator can safely hold.

There are laws to stop people from doing things in public that bother other people. Most towns have laws about being drunk in public and against begging. Every city or town has laws against **disturbing the peace**. Disturbing the peace is bothering other people. Noisy parties, loud music late at night, and fights can disturb the peace of a neighborhood.

There are also local laws to protect people's property. **Trespassing** laws keep people from entering someone else's house, office, or land without permission. **Vandalism** laws keep other people from destroying things that belong to someone else. Most towns have vandalism laws that protect government buildings and property.

Making Local Laws

Remember
Local laws are made in a similar way to state and federal laws.

The members of a county board or city council have important jobs. They make laws for their county, town, or city. The laws of a town may change the lives of a few hundred people. The laws of a large city may change the way millions of people do things. The city leaders are always elected by the people of the city. Elected lawmakers must make laws that are good for the people. If not, they may lose their jobs in the next election.

Ideas for new local laws are usually brought up by a board or council member during a meeting. The other members think it over and debate it. Is the law really necessary? How much will it cost? Will the law take away more rights than it protects? Finally, the council or board members vote. In some cities, the mayor can veto a new law. Usually, the council or board can override the veto by a two-thirds majority.

✓ Check Your Understanding

1. List two reasons why we have local laws.

2. Name one kind of local law, and describe what it does.

Taking Part in Local Government

Suppose you have an idea for a new local law to improve your community. Maybe you want a lower speed limit on your street so that children will be safer when they walk to school. Perhaps you want stronger laws to cut down on street crime. There are four ways you can get an idea for a new law passed in your community.

1. **Vote.** Support council members who support your idea for the law. Work to get those people elected.

2. **Talk to your council member.** Who represents you in the city council? This person usually lives nearby and knows your neighborhood well. You and your neighbors should tell your council member what you need.

3. **Attend or speak at council meetings.** You can attend council meetings at which new laws are made. Sometimes, local citizens can speak at the meetings. They can explain why a law should or

Government Fact

People have more power on the local level than in any other level of government.

should not be passed. Only the council members can vote. However, what a citizen says sometimes changes how they vote.

4. **Sign petitions.** You can use petitions. Some petitions—such as recalls, initiatives, and referendums—have legal power. You could sign an initiative to outlaw large trucks on neighborhood streets. You could sign a recall petition to get rid of a council member who is doing a poor job.

Remember
The U.S. Constitution, in the First Amendment, gives people the right to petition the government.

Other petitions do not have legal power. They only ask the council to do something. Council members usually carefully consider any petition that is signed by a great many people.

Some large cities, such as San Francisco and Los Angeles, have taken major steps to help solve their smog problems.

GOVERNMENT ISSUES
Clean Air in Los Angeles

Large cities in our country often have pollution problems. In the Los Angeles-Long Breach metropolitan area, the air was so dirty that it could have become a danger to people's health. On the worst days, children had to be kept from playing outdoors. The millions of cars, trucks, and buses caused part of the problem. Factories that gave off smoke and gases also contributed to the pollution. In 1989, the Los Angeles area had 222 days when the air quality was poor. The Air Quality Management District came up with a plan to clean up the air. The plan would change the way many people live and work.

The first steps proposed a change in the kinds of paints and thinners people can use in homes, in factories, and in construction. The plan called for all people to cut down on driving. It even called for new companies to be built closer to population centers. Furthermore, all cars will be required to use clean gases. Clean gases burn so that no extra gas escapes into the air.

All these steps could be very costly. People might have to buy more expensive cars. They might have to change their homes and offices. Painting buildings and making furniture would be more difficult. Paint companies, construction companies, and furniture manufacturers would probably be unhappy about the laws. However, clean air is important for everyone.

The plan has worked. In 1997, the Los Angeles metropolitan area had only 63 days when the air quality was unhealthy.

You Decide

Do you live in Los Angeles? If not, suppose you did. Would you and your family be willing to make the changes called for by the clean air law? Who do you think should pay for clean air?

Chapter

15 ▶ Review

Summary

Local laws are made to protect the rights and property of citizens. Many local laws limit what the people in a community can do.

Citizens may take part in local government. Ideas for local laws may be proposed by people in the community.

There are four basic ways for citizens to get laws passed by a council. (1) Vote for members who support your idea for a certain law. (2) Talk to your current council representative about the law you favor. (3) Attend or speak at council meetings in favor of the law. (4) Sign petitions that either can have the force of law or will put enough pressure on council members to vote for it.

trespass

property

disturbing the peace

vandalism

Vocabulary Review

Write a term from the list that matches each definition below.

1. Breaking a store window on purpose

2. Screaming, or playing loud music

3. A diamond ring, a house, a farm

4. To enter uninvited onto someone else's property

Chapter Quiz

Write your answers in complete sentences.

1. What is the purpose of local laws?

2. What are two local laws that protect the safety of citizens in a community?

3. What local law takes away someone's right in order to protect the rights of the whole community?

4. What is disturbing the peace?

5. What is vandalism?

6. Why do elected leaders have the power to make laws for large cities?

7. The purpose of most local laws is to protect two things. What are they?

8. What are four ways that citizens can take part in local government?

9. Critical Thinking What do you consider to be a local law that places too many limits on individual rights? Give your reasons.

10. Critical Thinking Why would council members pay attention to a petition that did not have the force of law?

Write About Government

Complete the following activity.

Write down two of your town's local laws. Then answer the following questions for each law.

1. Do you think the law is useful? Why or why not?

2. Does the law affect you and your family? How?

3. What problem or problems do you think each law was created to solve?

4. What do you think the strengths and weak points of each law are? Explain in detail.

You probably will need to do some research to answer questions 3 and 4. Ask your teacher or librarian for help.

This witness is sworn in during a trial in a local court.

Learning Objectives

- Identify the different kinds of local courts, and describe the cases they handle.
- Explain the rights of arrested persons.
- Describe the process of jury duty.

Words to Know

municipal court	the name of the local court in most cities
justice court	county court that handles criminal cases
misdemeanor	a small crime for which the sentence is a fine or less than one year in a local jail
fine	money paid after breaking a local law, such as a traffic law; sometimes, people can pay fines instead of going to jail
arrested	taken to jail by a law officer
arraignment	a hearing before a judge during which a person accused of a crime hears the charges against him or her
bail	money paid by a person to get out of jail before the trial; bail money pays for a bond, or written promise, that the accused will appear for trial
obligation	a duty or responsibility

Local Courts and Their Cases

Every city and county has local courts. In a city, the main local courts are usually called **municipal courts.** Outside the city, the local courts may be called **justice courts** or county courts. These courts are really the lowest courts of the state court system. They are called local courts because they take cases concerning local laws and problems. Local courts handle both civil and criminal cases.

Civil cases The municipal or county courts handle many kinds of civil cases. Divorce courts or family law courts settle cases for married people who break up. They also handle cases of people who want to adopt children. Probate courts settle questions about the property of a person who has died. Small claims court settles cases between people over small amounts of money or goods.

Criminal cases Local courts hold criminal trials only for **misdemeanor** crimes. Misdemeanors are small crimes. The sentence for a misdemeanor has to be less than one year in the local jail. Shoplifting and disturbing the peace are misdemeanors. Traffic courts handle cases of violations of local traffic laws. Speeding and parking tickets are handled by traffic courts. If a young person is on trial, the case is usually heard in juvenile court. Justice courts handle criminal cases in small towns and counties.

Small Claims Courts

Suppose you bought a new video game from a friend. Yet, when you got home to play it, it did not work. You want your money back. However, your friend refuses to take back the video. In most states, you can take such a case to a small claims court.

Small claims courts handle cases quickly. The court is often busy with many cases. You might have to wait a few weeks for your case to come up. When it does, it may take only 15 minutes to settle. Small claims court cases move quickly because juries are not allowed and the use of lawyers is discouraged. Instead, each person tells his or her story directly to the judge. The judge listens and asks questions. Then the judge decides who is in the wrong and what that person must pay. In most states, the claim has to be for $5,000 or less. Small claims cases can usually be appealed.

✓ **Check Your Understanding**

1. What are the local courts in a city called?

2. What kind of case does a probate court handle?

Traffic Court

Traffic court is another very busy court. Every day, people get tickets for breaking local traffic laws. Speeding, blocking traffic, and careless driving are all violations of local traffic laws. Sometimes, the guilty person has to pay only a **fine,** such as $35 for a parking ticket. Sometimes, the accused must appear in traffic court.

Most traffic court cases have no lawyers and no jury. The driver and the police officer who issued the ticket appear before a judge. The police officer and the driver both tell their stories. The judge asks questions and makes the decision. A driver who is found guilty can appeal. Yet, few do. A traffic court sentence is often just a fine. Hiring an appeal lawyer may cost more than paying the fine.

Rights of Arrested Persons

Most people who break local laws are not **arrested** or held by the police. Police officers write them a ticket for speeding or for disturbing the peace. They may be told to pay a fine. If they want to argue the case, they may be given a date to appear in court before a judge.

Some local crimes call for arrests. A person can be arrested for misdemeanors such as vandalism, shoplifting, or drunk driving. When a person is arrested, his or her right to freedom can be taken away. However, many rights are still protected, both by the state and federal constitutions. The police and the courts must be careful to protect the rights of citizens and treat them fairly.

You will read about many of these rights in later chapters in this book. The following are three basic rights of arrested persons that must be protected by the local police and courts.

1. **The right to stay silent** People who are arrested do not *have* to answer any questions. Furthermore, they cannot be found guilty just because they refuse to answer questions. The Constitution promises that people must be considered innocent until a trial. Only after they are proven guilty in court can they be considered guilty.

2. **The right to have a lawyer** Anyone accused of a crime has the right to a lawyer. If a person does not have enough money for a lawyer, he or she must be given one for free. The state or local government pays for the lawyer.

3. **The right to appear quickly before a judge** Usually, an arrested person first appears before a judge at a hearing, called an **arraignment.** The person must be told for what crimes he or she has been arrested. The accused also gets the chance to tell the judge whether he is innocent or guilty.

Also at this first hearing, the judge can set **bail.** The smaller the crime, the lower the bail. People who pay the bail must be set free until their trial begins. People out on bail who do not show up for trial lose their bail money. The bail money acts as a promise that people will appear for trial and not run away.

These same rights are guaranteed to people who face trial in state or federal courts. In local courts, the crimes and the sentences are less serious than those in state and federal courts. A person's right to a fair trial is just as important. These rights are strongly protected, no matter how serious the case is.

Government Fact

Sometimes, in very serious crimes, the judge can refuse to set bail. Then the accused is held in jail until the trial.

Citizenship and You

JURY DUTY

One **obligation** of being a U.S. citizen is serving on a jury. Almost all citizens are called to serve one or more times on a jury during their lives.

If you are signed up as a voter or have a driver's license, you might be called to serve on a jury. If you are called, you will get a legal notice from the local courthouse. You must answer the notice and report to court. The notice tells you when to appear. You might have to be on call for two weeks or as long as three months in some states. You and other jurors wait to be assigned to a case. When you are a possible juror, the lawyers for each side may ask you questions. One lawyer may not want you to be on the jury. He or she can ask that you be excused.

Before the trial can begin, the lawyers must agree on 12 jurors. If you get to serve on a jury, you will hear one case. The case might take a few days, a few weeks, or, in some cases, a few months. You have to go to court every day until the trial is over. The judge will warn you each night not to talk about the case outside of court. At the end of the case, the judge gives you the rules for making a decision. You and the other jurors go into a closed room to vote in secret. The secret meeting goes on until all 12 people agree on the case. In criminal cases, the jury must vote guilty or not guilty. If the vote is guilty, the judge will usually decide the sentence. In a civil case, the jury decides who wins the disagreement between the private parties. The jury may also decide how much money should be paid to the person who wins the case.

Your jury duty is over for the time being. You can be called again to serve, but probably not for a few years.

You Decide

Why does the government make it an obligation for citizens to serve on juries?

Chapter
16 ▶ Review

Summary

Local courts handle small civil and criminal cases. Municipal courts are city courts, and justice courts are county courts.
Local courts hold criminal trials only for misdemeanor crimes. Traffic courts handle violations of local traffic laws. Juvenile courts handle cases involving young people.
Most people accused of breaking local laws are not arrested. For some misdemeanors, the accused person can be arrested. An arrested person still has basic rights as a citizen.
Small claims courts can handle civil cases quickly. There are no lawyers or a jury. The judge hears both sides of the case and then reaches a decision.

arraignment
arrested
justice court
bail
municipal court

Vocabulary Review

Complete each sentence with a term from the list.

1. A local court is called a _____.

2. A judge reads the charges against a person on trial at an _____.

3. A _____ is where criminals are tried.

4. When people post _____, they guarantee that they will be in court for their trial.

5. When people are caught committing a crime, they are _____.

Chapter Quiz

Write your answers in complete sentences.

1. What kinds of cases does a family law court handle?

2. What kinds of cases does a probate court handle?

3. What are two misdemeanor crimes?

4. Why are small claims cases settled so quickly?

5. What is the usual penalty for a guilty person in a traffic court case?

6. What two things happen at an arraignment?

7. Critical Thinking Why do you think the rights of people who are arrested are so carefully guarded? Explain your reasons.

8. Critical Thinking How does the size of the jury help assure all defendants a fair trial?

Write About Government

Complete the following activity.

Look at the cases described below. Write the numbers 1–4 on a sheet of paper. Next to each number, write the name of the court that will probably hear the case.

1. A married couple wants to adopt a child.

2. A woman dies. Her three surviving relatives have a disagreement over who is entitled to her property.

3. A man's tree falls on his neighbor's fence. The fence owner wants the neighbor to pay $600 to have it fixed.

4. A 13-year-old boy is arrested for destroying the window of a jewelry store.

Unit 3 **Review**

Comprehension Check
Complete the sentences by choosing the correct word or phrase.

1. The highest law in each state is the state's (orders from the governor/constitution).

2. The states have the power to protect the health, well-being, and (money/safety) of their people.

3. Members of state legislatures are elected from (assessors/districts).

4. A proposal for a state law that comes directly from the people is called (a recall/an initiative).

5. A major difference between the powers of the President and those of a governor is (a governor must share executive power/a governor cannot draw up a budget).

6. The lowest courts in the state court system are the (courts of appeals/trial courts).

7. The local government official responsible for deciding the amount of tax paid on land and property is the (county clerk/county assessor).

8. Disturbing the peace is an example of (an arraignment/a misdemeanor).

Writing an Essay
Answer one of the following essay topics.

1. Discuss the importance of having three different levels of government—the federal, state, and local.

2. Explain five similarities between state governments and the federal government.

3. Discuss the different structures of city government.

Government in Your Life
Which local government services does your school use? Discuss how these services affect you and your classmates.

Your Freedoms as Americans

Judaism is one of many religions practiced in the United States.

Learning Objectives

- Describe the history of religious freedom in America.

- Explain why religious freedom is important.

- List the principles behind the idea of religious freedom in the United States today.

Words to Know

official	having the power of the government; an official religion is one set up and run by the government
persecute	to harm over and over again; to treat people badly because of their beliefs or ideas
religious persecution	unfair treatment of people because of the religion they practice
private	not run by the government
voluntary	done by a person's own choosing or free will

The History of Religious Freedom in the United States

Most of this country's first settlers were from England, France, Spain, and other countries in Europe. Many of those countries had **official** religions. People who did not belong to the official religion were often **persecuted**. They were denied many of the same rights as other citizens. They were put in jail, sometimes even killed. For this reason, many of them fled from their homelands.

People who came to North America wanted freedom from this **religious persecution**. However, in the early years of settlement, several colonies set up their own official religions. All people had to attend the same church. They had to help pay for the official religion. People who did not belong to the official religion were carefully watched by the government. In some places, people who did not belong to the official religion could not own land.

By the time the United States became a country, there were dozens of different religions spread throughout the states. Each had its own group of followers. Each group wanted freedom for itself and feared persecution by other groups. To protect all groups in all states fairly, religious freedom had to be promised by the new government. Some states already had constitutions that promised religious freedom. These ideas were made part of the U.S. Constitution.

Why Religious Freedom Is Important

Why is religious freedom important? The following story might give you some idea of what could happen without religious freedom.

History Fact

Many countries still have official religions, but most allow people to follow religions of their choice.

What If There Were an Official Church?

Suppose one day, the federal government set up an official church called the Church of the United States. Everyone who worked for the government had to join the church. Other citizens could join the church if they wanted. However, all citizens had to help pay for the church.

The Roberts family already belonged to a different church. In school, the Roberts children had to learn the beliefs of the Church of the United States. They began each day with an official prayer. They spent one hour a day in a Church of the United States religion class. Science classes were changed to teach only what the church leaders allowed. Children who belonged to the official church got to take special trips and classes. Other children did not.

More and more people joined the Church of the United States. The members of the U.S. church began to look down on all those who were

members of other churches. One day, Bobby
Roberts came home with a bloody nose. He had
gotten into a fight with some other students
about religion.

Then one day, Mrs. Roberts lost her government
job. The police began to ask the Roberts's neighbors
questions about the Roberts family. A few months
later, Congress passed two new laws. Only church
members could go to public schools. Worst of all,
all people who did not belong to the Church of the
United States had to leave the country.

The members of the Roberts family were
heartbroken. They had to choose between the
beliefs they loved or the country they loved. How
could they ever be happy or free again?

This story is frightening. However, it will never
happen in this country. That is because of the
guarantees of religious freedom written into the
U.S. Constitution.

✓ Check Your Understanding

1. Why did so many Europeans come to North
   America to settle?

2. Why did the framers of the U.S. Constitution
   include guarantees of religious freedom in the
   document they wrote?

The Laws About Freedom of Religion

The First Amendment of the Constitution
guarantees freedom of religion. What does that mean?
Supreme Court cases over the years have made the
meaning of the First Amendment clearer. State and

Remember
The first 10 amendments to
the Constitution are called
the Bill of Rights.

local laws have added to this idea. Today, we understand that religious freedom in the United States is based on the following principles.

- **The government cannot set up an official religion.** Religion and government must be kept apart.

- **The government cannot favor any religion through special laws, money, or other help.** **Private** Americans or private groups can favor a religion. Private schools can teach religion. They are not supported by the government. Public schools, which are paid for by the government, cannot teach religion. If they did, the government would be helping one religion without helping all the others.

The United States is a representative democracy. The government must represent all its people, not just a few. There are at least 175 different religious groups in the United States. What if the government officially supported only the Catholic religion? Then it could not fairly represent the millions of people who are Baptists or Episcopalians or Muslims. Public schools can teach information *about* religions. They can teach about the Bible or the Koran. They can teach about religious ideas of different countries. However, they cannot teach students how or what to believe.

- **People may believe in any religions they want—or none at all.** Other people cannot force you to believe what they believe. You cannot be forced to give up your own beliefs. Your boss cannot fire you because of your religion. Your school cannot force you to leave because of your religion. In addition, no one can force you to move because of your religion.

- **A religion's rules cannot violate the law.** If a state law says that children must attend school until the eighth grade, it means *all* children. Suppose the rules of one religion say 10-year-olds should leave school to work for the church. The government says they cannot. All children must stay in school until the eighth grade.

Government Skills

MAIN IDEAS AND SUPPORTING DETAILS

Earlier in this book, you learned some ways to study. One of the best ways is to remember the different points or main ideas. The learning objectives at the beginning of each chapter are important points to remember. Often, the blue headings within the chapter also name the main ideas.

Under each heading are facts, or supporting details. Together, the supporting details explain the main idea. Sometimes, the supporting details are in a story that shows how an idea works. Sometimes, the details are a list of facts. In government, it may be a list of laws.

1. On a separate sheet of paper, list the main ideas for this chapter.

2. Look for supporting details for each main idea. Under each main idea, list at least two supporting details.

LANDMARK CHANGES IN THE LAW
Bible-Reading in Public Schools

In 1963, a Pennsylvania law required that all public schools begin each school day with a reading from the Bible. Students would say the Lord's Prayer together and then salute the flag.

The members of the Schempp family belonged to the Unitarian church. However, they believed that the Bible-readings and prayers were unfair to their children. They felt that their children should not be forced to follow a religion against their will. They also believed that a public school was not the right place for religious practices. They complained to the school.

The school did not agree. It said the Bible was an important part of American life. It also said that reading and praying helped to make the students better people. Finally, the school pointed out, these religious acts were **voluntary.** If a student's parents wanted, the student could leave the classroom during the Bible-reading and prayer. Therefore, the school claimed, no religion was being forced on anyone's children.

However, the Schempps were not satisfied. They thought their children might be picked on if they left the classroom. They feared that their children might be persecuted by other children for being different. The Schempps felt that their children had lost their freedom of religion. The Schempps asked the Supreme Court to hear their case. They argued that Bible-reading and praying in school was against the Constitution.

The Supreme Court ruled in favor of the Schempps in *School District of Abingdon Township, Pennsylvania* v. *Schempp.* The Court said that the school had taken away the Schempp children's freedom of religion. Furthermore, the Court said, the state law violated the First Amendment to the Constitution. By requiring students to read from the Bible, the state government was favoring one religion over another.

Public schools are for children of all religions. Public schools are paid for by people of all religions. The government that runs those schools cannot favor one religion over another. The Court ordered the public schools to stop all Bible-reading and prayers.

You Decide

Suppose you were a Supreme Court justice in the *Schempp* case. Would you have decided for or against the Schempps? Why?

The Schempp family went to court to fight for their religious freedom.

Summary

Many of the first settlers to come to North America came from countries that had official religions. These settlers came to avoid religious persecution. The first colonies set up their own official religions.

The idea of religious freedom was written into the U.S. Constitution. The First Amendment to the Constitution guarantees freedom of religion.

Vocabulary Review

Write *true* or *false*. If the statement is false, change the underlined term to make it true.

1. The <u>private</u> flag of the United States is designated by the government.

2. Some people who fled Europe to settle the colonies in North America were escaping <u>religious persecution</u>.

3. If someone chooses to do something, he or she is performing a <u>voluntary</u> act.

4. When something does not involve the government, it is considered an <u>official</u> issue.

5. To <u>persecute</u> people is to treat them badly because of their ideas and beliefs.

Chapter Quiz

Write your answers in complete sentences.

1. What countries did the early European settlers to North America come from?

2. How were the European settlers who came to North America persecuted before they left their native lands?

3. What kinds of rules did the people in colonies with official religions have to follow?

4. Why did the new government under the U.S. Constitution have to guarantee freedom of religion?

5. Where did the ideas of freedom of religion written into the Constitution originally come from?

6. About how many different religious groups are there in the United States today?

7. Why is religion not taught in public schools?

8. What are public schools allowed to teach about religion?

9. **Critical Thinking** What has helped make the laws on religious freedom clearer in meaning?

10. **Critical Thinking** Why did the Supreme Court order public schools to stop all Bible reading and prayers?

Write About Government

Complete the following activity.

What does the idea of religious freedom mean to you? How would the lives of you and your family be different if the United States denied people freedom of religion or freedom from religion?

Chapter 18

Freedom of Speech and Press

Freedom of the press includes the right of the press to question and criticize the government and its leaders. President Ronald Reagan met often with the press during his presidency.

Learning Objectives

- Name a historic case of freedom of the press.
- Explain why freedom of speech and freedom of the press are important.
- Describe the protections and limits of freedom of speech.
- Describe the protections and limits of freedom of the press.

Words to Know

criticize	to point out what is wrong with something
express	to say or show what you think or feel
information	facts; knowledge given or received
slander	to say something untrue about someone in order to do harm to that person
prior restraint	an order to prevent a person from doing something
libel	to write or broadcast something untrue about someone in order to harm that person
obscene	something that offends the public sense of decency
protest	to disagree strongly

A Historic Case of Freedom of the Press

Suppose you ran a newspaper. Could you be arrested for printing the truth in your paper?

In 1734, the American colonies were still under British rule. In that year, a newspaper called the *New York Weekly Journal* printed stories that criticized the local British government. The publisher of the paper was a man named John Peter Zenger. He was arrested and thrown in jail for writing these stories. At his trial, Zenger tried to show that the stories were true. However, the judge would not allow him to do so. At that time, *any* stories that criticized the government were against the law. It did not matter if the stories were true.

Then something amazing happened. A jury of local people went against the judge. The jury set Zenger free because they were convinced he had printed the truth.

The jury believed people had a right to speak the truth. In addition, they believed that people had the right to criticize their government.

John Peter Zenger had printed the truth. In 1734, he barely escaped going to jail for a long time. In the United States today, the First Amendment promises freedom of the press and freedom of speech to all Americans.

Why Freedom of Speech and Freedom of the Press Are Important

The United States is a representative democracy. That means the people of the country hold the final power. The people choose representatives. The representatives pass laws that the people want. The people must have new ideas to help govern the country. To do this, freedom of speech and press are necessary.

With freedom of speech and freedom of the press, people can **express** most ideas in public. They do not have to fear being stopped by the government.

Freedom of speech and press also help people get good **information**. People need facts and ideas before deciding what to do. The country faces many problems. Usually, there are a number of possible answers to the problems. Each possible answer probably has some strong points and some weak points. A free press helps bring out all the facts, both good and bad. It also brings out many different ideas, both good and bad.

Why is it important to protect this right? It is easy to listen to the ideas of the majority. People who agree with the government do not need protection. Their ideas will be easily heard by others and by the leaders of the country. What about those who disagree or whose ideas are unpopular? These people need their freedoms of speech and press protected most.

Their ideas are important, too. After all, sometimes good ideas are very unpopular at first.

In the 1760s, not many people in the American colonies wanted to separate from Great Britain. By 1776, however, the idea had grown into a war for independence. When the Constitution was written, the idea of freeing slaves was unpopular in several states. The idea of allowing minority groups and women the right to vote was unpopular. Later, these ideas became part of the Constitution. None of these ideas would have been heard without freedom of speech or the press. Each of those ideas had the power to change our lives.

✓ **Check Your Understanding**

1. Who was John Peter Zenger? Why is he important to the history of free press?

2. List two reasons why freedom of speech and freedom of press are important.

Freedom of Speech: Protections and Limits

The First Amendment clearly states what the government cannot do. It says that the government cannot pass any law that takes away the freedom of speech. What does that mean the people *can* do?

Protections First, you can speak freely without being arrested or stopped. You can say what you believe is true, even if you are wrong. You can talk about your ideas, even if they are unpopular. You can criticize the government and its leaders.

Second, the Supreme Court has said that freedom of speech covers more than just speaking. You are free to express your ideas by what you do. You can write, make signs or pictures, join a march, wave a flag. Those acts are protected just as much as the spoken word.

Remember
The Supreme Court made an important ruling about free speech. Turn back to Chapter 9 to review it.

Third, you are free to make your ideas public. You can talk on the radio, on television, on the Internet, or in public places. You can speak in parks, on street corners, and in indoor or outdoor arenas.

Limits The Supreme Court has also placed some limits on free speech. First, you cannot use free speech to break a law. For example, you cannot lie to cheat people out of their money. Second, you cannot **slander** other people—say things you know are not true in order to hurt them. Third, you cannot say things you know are not true if they put others in danger. Suppose you yell *"Fire!"* is a crowded room when there was really no fire. The rush to escape could hurt or kill people. You are not free to do such things.

These limits on free speech do allow for honest mistakes. Suppose you make a speech. You claim that a city council member has been stealing money from the city. Later, it turns out that you were wrong. The city council member takes you to court for slander. If you can prove you honestly believed what you claimed, you are protected. If the city council member can prove you knew your speech was not true, you are not protected. You can be found guilty of slander.

One limit the Supreme Court has not placed on free speech is that of **prior restraint.** Suppose someone in government thinks you are *going* to break a law. Your right to speak cannot be taken away for something you have not yet done. Suppose the city council member thought you were *about* to slander one of its members. The council cannot do anything until you speak. Then, if you *do* slander a council member, you can be taken to court.

Freedom from prior restraint is important to free speech and free press. Otherwise, the government might persecute you for the ideas it just imagines that you hold. That is not freedom.

Government Fact

The standard used for deciding the limit of free speech is called the "clear and present danger doctrine."

Freedom of the Press: Protections and Limits

Protections Freedom of the press protects newspapers, magazines, and radio and television stations. It protects writers, artists, and those who make films. These organizations and groups all have the same rights as anyone else. They can criticize the government. They can print the truth as they see it. They can print new or unpopular ideas. They are free to make honest mistakes.

Limits Newspapers and other press organizations face the same limits as other Americans. They cannot **libel** people on purpose. Libel is a way of slandering someone in print. Freedom of speech is limited by laws against slander. Freedom of the press is limited by laws against libel as well. If a person feels he or she has been libeled, that person can go to court to try and prove it. However, as in cases that involve slander, he or she must prove the libel was done on purpose.

There are also limits on press freedom in regard to national security. No press organization can publish or broadcast anything that could hurt the defense of the country.

The final limit on press freedom has to do with **obscene** material. This area is one of great disagreement. What one person considers obscene, another may not. In general, the courts have used the guideline of *community standards*. If printed or broadcast material does not offend the average person in the community, it is not obscene.

> **You Decide**
>
> Can a statement be libel if it is truthful? What did the jury in the Zenger case decide on this issue?

✓ Check Your Understanding

1. Describe two protections under freedom of speech.

2. What is slander?

LANDMARK CHANGES IN THE LAW
Free Speech at School

In 1965, the United States was fighting the Vietnam War. Back home, Americans had strong disagreements about the war. Many people were against the war. They said the United States had no reason to be in Vietnam. Other people said America *had* to fight the war. They said fighting in Vietnam was necessary to protect the free world.

In December 1965, three students in Des Moines, Iowa, decided to **protest** the war. Mary Beth Tinker, her brother John, and their friend Christopher Eckhardt wore black armbands to their schools. They wore the armbands to show that they were against the war in Vietnam. They carried no signs and made no speeches. They only wore the armbands in a silent protest.

The school officials knew that the students were planning to wear the armbands beforehand. They held a meeting to decide what to do.

The officials believed that school was no place for a protest. They believed students were in school to learn and had to follow school rules. They decided to send home any students who wore armbands. When the three students showed up at school, they were sent home.

The Tinker and Eckhardt parents thought this action was unfair. They took the school to court. They explained that the students had caused no trouble. They also said that the students had a right to free speech guaranteed by the First Amendment.

The school officials answered that their job was to keep order during school hours. They said they had a right to stop anything that might cause trouble in classes. The students were in school to learn, not to protest.

This case went all the way to the Supreme Court. The Court had some tricky things to decide. First, the students were not adults. Did they have the same protection as adults under the First Amendment? Second, a school usually has the right to make its own rules about how students can act in school. Did that right hold up in this case? Third, a school usually has the right to stop any trouble from happening in class. Did the school not have the right to stop trouble before it started?

The Supreme Court ruled in favor of the Tinkers in *Tinker* v. *Des Moines Independent Community School District* (1969). The Court said that students were protected by the First Amendment, even at school. Their right to free speech did not end when they set foot on school grounds. The Court agreed that schools have the right to stop trouble in classes. It agreed that the armbands might have caused trouble. However, said the Court, the chance of trouble is not a strong enough reason to take away freedom of speech.

You Decide

Do you think it is more important to allow free speech or to keep peace on school grounds? Explain your answer.

In 1969, the U.S. Supreme Court ruled that the Tinker children had a right to protest the Vietnam War at school.

Summary

Freedom of the press had its beginnings in colonial America in 1734.

Freedom of speech and freedom of the press are important to Americans for many reasons. People need to express ideas freely if they are to take part in government.

The First Amendment guarantees certain protections in the area of free speech. The Supreme Court has placed certain limits on free speech.

Freedom of the press protects newspapers, magazines, and radio and television stations. It also protects writers, artists, and filmmakers. There are limits on freedom of the press.

criticize
libel
express
slander
obscene

Vocabulary Review

Write the term from the list that matches each definition below.

1. To point out flaws in an argument

2. To spread false information to hurt others

3. To show how you feel about something

4. Something that is considered indecent

5. False information that is printed to harm another person

Chapter Quiz

Write your answers in complete sentences.

1. Why was John Peter Zenger found not guilty?

2. Why are freedom of speech and freedom of the press important in a representative democracy like the United States?

3. What two unpopular ideas later became part of the U.S. Constitution?

4. What are the three major protections under the right to free speech?

5. What is an example of slander?

6. How can a person accused of slander show that he or she is not guilty?

7. What is prior restraint?

8. What is the difference between libel and slander?

9. **Critical Thinking** How do freedom of speech and freedom of the press help people get information?

10. **Critical Thinking** What is an example of something a newspaper might publish that could hurt the national security? Explain your answer.

Write About Government

Complete the following activity.

How does freedom of speech and freedom of the press affect your community? Do you know of a local case in which someone has been accused of violating limits on free speech or a free press? Would you be in favor of your school newspaper printing something that could upset your school or community? Why or why not?

Dr. Martin Luther King, Jr. (center), and his supporters often used freedom of assembly to fight for equal opportunity for African Americans.

Learning Objectives

- Explain how the First Amendment guarantees the freedom of assembly and freedom to petition.

- Explain why freedom of assembly and freedom to petition are important in a representative democracy.

- Describe the protections and limitations of freedom of assembly.

- Describe the protections and limits of freedom to petition.

Words to Know

assemble	to gather or meet together; an **assembly** is a gathering of people
organize	to join in a group in order to work together
picket line	a group of people who protest something by marching in front of a building and carrying signs
violent	showing or acting with strong force that causes harm
unofficial	having no legal power
riot	an out-of-control fight among many people

Organizing for Change

Suppose you think the police chief in your town is doing a bad job. You think the chief should be fired. You talk to your neighbors. They think so too. If these people agree with you, maybe others will as well.

You want to talk over your idea with other people in the town. You decide to have an open meeting at the town hall. You hope everyone there will sign a petition. The petition will ask the city council to fire the police chief. After all, the city government is supposed to work for the people. If enough people want something, the city government should follow their wishes.

Your neighbors say they will not go to any public meeting. They think the police chief will not allow it. In addition, they are afraid the chief will arrest anyone who signs the petition.

Can the police chief stop the meeting and arrest people for signing the petition? In some countries, he or she might be able to. However, in the United States, the First Amendment guarantees the people the freedom to **assemble** and freedom to petition.

Freedom of assembly means that groups of people can meet peaceably whenever they want. People can hold public or private meetings to talk about their ideas and problems. They can **organize** themselves to work together. They can plan to work for changes.

Freedom to petition means that people can ask their government, in writing, to take some action. People sign their names to the petition. Then the government can see how many people support the idea. The freedoms of assembly and petition give people the right to take part in—and sometimes change—their government.

Why Freedom of Assembly Is Important

Your right to speak freely is guaranteed by the Constitution. However, it would not mean very much unless you can tell others your ideas and problems. You then learn new ideas by listening to others. Furthermore, only if you have the right to assemble can you make plans to solve the problems.

Freedom of assembly gives you the right to organize with others into a larger group. The United States is a representative democracy. Your local representative may speak for thousands of people. Alone, you may not have much power if you ask your representative to do something.

Have you ever heard the saying, "There is power in numbers"? The larger your group, the more likely your "group voice" will be heard. Suppose you have a thousand or more people in your group. You can be pretty sure your representative will listen to your ideas.

Why Freedom to Petition Is Important

The freedom to petition gives you the right to ask, in writing, for changes in government. It upholds the right of free speech and press. Suppose you make a speech. You criticize the city government for not having enough bus service. Many people agree with you. Yet, after the speech, no one in city government takes action. No one really knows how many people want more bus service. Suppose you write a petition and 30,000 people sign it. The people in government can read the petition. They can see that 30,000 people want more bus service. In that case, the government is much more likely to add more buses.

Freedom of Assembly: Protections and Limits

Protections The First Amendment gives people the right to hold any assembly, or meeting—that is, as long as the meeting is peaceful and has no illegal purpose. No state or local government can pass laws against such meetings. No one can stop people from going to meetings. In addition, no one can arrest people for attending meetings.

The Supreme Court has made the First Amendment clearer by deciding many cases about freedom of assembly. It has decided that the right of assembly covers more than just meetings. It also protects **picket lines**. Workers fighting for higher pay may stay off work and march in a picket line. The First Amendment protects marches, such as those used by people protesting the Vietnam War. It also protects other kinds of peaceful gatherings.

People must be allowed to assemble in public places. Any group can meet in public meeting rooms, city parks, or streets. Shopping mall owners must let

Remember
In Chapter 11, you read about initiatives, referendums, and recalls. Each is a kind of petition that people can use to make new laws, stop new laws, or remove people from office.

people assemble in the open parts of the malls. Like free speech, free assembly would mean very little if it could not be done in public.

Local governments must also protect the people who assemble. Suppose some people march against having a new shopping center built. Many other people might be in favor of the new center and become angry at the marchers. The local government must protect the marchers from harm or persecution.

Limits There are some constitutional limits on freedom of assembly. No one has the right to assemble for any illegal purpose, such as robbery or vandalism. The police can stop a **violent** assembly, or one that tries to lead people to violent acts.

A local government can put some limits on assembly in public places. It can make sure that marches, picket lines, and other assemblies stay peaceful. It can also make sure that these assemblies do not block traffic or keep people from getting to stores and offices. It can make fire safety rules that say how many people can gather safely in a meeting room. In addition, it can set fees for people who want to hold marches, meetings, or otherwise use land or buildings. All these limits and fees must be reasonable.

Freedom of Petition: Protections and Limits

There are two kinds of petitions. In Chapter 11, you learned about referendums, recalls, and initiatives. These kinds of petitions have legal power. If enough people sign them, the government has to follow through on what the petitions ask. The other kind of petition is **unofficial**. It has no legal power. You read about unofficial petition on page 229. The petition for more bus service did not have legal power. When enough people sign an unofficial petition, the government is wise to notice and take action. If not, the voters can choose a new set of representatives to lead them.

Protections The freedom to petition is also protected by the Constitution and by "case law" from Supreme Court decisions. You are guaranteed the right to sign petitions. You also have the right to go to public places to ask people to sign your petition.

Limits There are some limits on the freedom to petition. Usually, petitions must follow a set form. The rules must be followed, or the petition is no good. People who sign a petition must write their full names and addresses. They must live in the town or city where the petition was written. Furthermore, they can only sign it once. In some places, only registered voters can sign a petition.

Government Fact

A town clerk or city attorney can supply the petition rules for your town or city.

✓ **Check Your Understanding**

1. Why would the right to free speech not mean much without the freedom to assemble?

2. Name one protection and one limit on the freedom to assemble.

LANDMARK CHANGES IN THE LAW
Protecting Peaceful Marchers

In Chapter 9, you read about *Brown* v. *Board of Education of Topeka* (1954). In that case, the Supreme Court decided that laws that set up separate schools for African American and white students were unconstitutional. Public schools were ordered to end such segregation as quickly as they could. However, ten years later, many schools in the country were still segregated.

In 1965, an entertainer and activist named Dick Gregory organized a number of people in Chicago. They said that the schools there were moving too slowly in ending segregation. Gregory and his followers formed a group to talk to the mayor of Chicago, Richard Daley. They asked him to hire a new superintendent for the public schools. They asked for someone who would end segregation more quickly. The people in the group decided to organize a march to show how they felt. About 85 of them marched from city hall to the mayor's home and formed a picket line.

Then a crowd of Daley's followers began to gather. The crowd grew to about 1,000 people. These people yelled and tried to scare the marchers to make them go away. The crowd of Mayor Daley's followers grew larger and became violent. They began throwing eggs and rocks at the marchers.

The Chicago police had been watching the marchers and the crowd. The head of the police began to fear that a **riot** might start. He asked the marchers to end their assembly and go home. The marchers answered that they were doing nothing wrong. They continued with their protest march.

The police said that the crowd of onlookers was getting very angry. They said they were afraid people might get hurt. The police then arrested Dick Gregory and many of his followers. The marchers were charged with breaking a Chicago city law. This law forbade any gathering that bothered other people or started riots.

The case was heard in a local Chicago court. The marchers pointed out that they had been peaceful. They said they had a right to freedom of assembly. They had a right to march in protest of segregation. The police said that their job was to keep peace and to keep people from getting hurt. They thought the marchers were going to cause a riot. The local court found the marchers guilty.

You Decide

Should the police be allowed to head off violence by stopping a peaceful march? If you were on the Supreme Court, what would you have decided? Explain your answer.

Some of the marchers took the case all the way to the Supreme Court. In 1969, the Court unanimously overturned the local court's ruling (*Gregory* v. *Chicago*). The Court agreed with the marchers that the march was protected by the First Amendment. The Court said that peaceful assembly was lawful. It noted that the police had a responsibility to keep peace and keep people safe. The Court also pointed out that the Daley supporters were causing trouble, not the marchers. It went on to say that the police had a responsibility to protect the marchers' right to assemble peaceably, even if their assembling annoyed others.

Chapter

19 ▷ Review

Summary

The First Amendment guarantees people the freedom to assemble and the freedom to petition. Freedom to assemble is the right of people to meet in groups to exchange ideas or even to criticize the government. Freedom to petition is the right of people to ask the government in writing to make changes.

There are both protections and limits on the freedom to assemble. Freedom to assemble covers picket lines, either in worker strikes or protest marches. Local governments must also protect people who assemble from harm or persecution. No one has a right to assemble for an illegal purpose or to encourage violent acts.

There are protections and limits on the freedom to petition. You are free to sign petitions and have the right to ask others to sign your petition.

violent
picket line
riot
assemble
unofficial

Vocabulary Review

Complete each sentence with a term from the list.

1. A _____ is a peaceful demonstration of protest.

2. To organize a protest, a leader might _____ a group of people.

3. A protest where people are out of control is called a _____.

4. Police can stop a _____ assembly.

5. If something is _____, it is without legal power.

Chapter Quiz

Write your answers in complete sentences.

1. Which amendment to the Constitution guarantees the freedom to assemble and the freedom to petition?

2. What are two protections of the freedom to assemble?

3. What is a picket line?

4. What are two limits on the freedom to assemble?

5. What are *legal* petitions? Give one example.

6. What is an *unofficial* petition? Give one example.

7. What is one limit on the freedom to petition?

8. What did the Supreme Court decide in the case of *Gregory* v. *Chicago*?

9. **Critical Thinking** What does the saying "There is power in numbers" mean?

10. **Critical Thinking** Does a petition have a better chance of getting government leaders to act than someone making a speech? Explain.

Write About Government

Complete the following activity.

Suppose you could get a petition signed by many people to change something in your town. What would you like to change? Why?

Unit 4 **Review**

Comprehension Check
Complete the sentences by choosing the correct word or phrase.

1. Many of the first settlers to America came to escape from (religious persecution/poor working conditions).

2. Religious freedom means people can (pray anytime in school/ believe or not believe in any religion).

3. John Peter Zenger won the right to (print anything he wanted in his newspaper/criticize the government if he told the truth).

4. Freedom of speech means that people can (speak their ideas in public/slander government officials).

5. One limit on freedom of the press is the (law against libel/law on prior restraint).

6. Freedom of assembly does *not* include the right to (encourage violent acts/assemble in parks).

7. An example of freedom of assembly is (a riot/a picket line).

8. Freedom to petition can be limited by (certain rules about the petition's form/the acts of a mayor).

Writing an Essay
Answer one of the following essay topics.

1. Explain the principles of religious freedom in the United States.

2. Discuss the limits on freedom of speech and freedom of the press in the United States.

3. Summarize how freedom of speech and freedom of assembly are linked to one another.

Government in Your Life
How would your life in this country be different if we did not have the freedoms of religion, speech, the press, and assembly and petition? Include two activities that you would not be permitted to do without these freedoms.

Chapter 20

Right to Equal Opportunity

James Meredith was the first African American to attend the University of Mississippi.

Learning Objectives

- Explain how the guarantees of equal protection and due process work together to guarantee equal opportunity.
- Explain how the laws and court cases have come to guarantee equal opportunity.

Words to Know

equal protection	receiving the same treatment under the law as everyone else
equal opportunity	receiving the same chance as everyone else to do or to have something
due process	the ways laws are carried out to protect people's rights
discrimination	the act of treating people unfairly
physical disability	an injury or problem with the body that keeps a person from moving, acting, or working the same way as able-bodied people
manager	a person whose job is to oversee a group of workers

The Idea of Equal Opportunity

One day in December 1955, a woman in Alabama stood waiting for a bus. Finally, the bus came. She climbed up the steps, paid her fare, and took the first empty seat.

The bus driver became angry. He told the woman she knew she could not sit there. She had to sit in the *back* of the bus. It was a city law.

The woman on the bus was named Rosa Parks. Rosa Parks was an African American woman living in Montgomery, Alabama. At that time, a Montgomery city law said that African American people could sit only in the back seats of city buses. However, on that day in 1955, Rosa Parks did not move to the back of the bus. She said she was tired of giving in to racism. She was later arrested and found guilty of breaking the city law.

Rosa Parks appealed her conviction. Eventually, her case went all the way to the Supreme Court. More than a year later, the Court overturned her conviction. The Court decided that Rosa Parks had as much right to take a front seat as anyone else. She was riding a public bus. The city law was unconstitutional. It violated the Fourteenth Amendment's guarantee of **equal protection** under the laws. She had a right to **equal opportunity** to sit in the front seats.

The Constitution does not mention the words "equal opportunity." However, the Fourteenth Amendment guarantees both **due process** and equal protection under the law. Due process means the government must always give you all your constitutional rights. Equal protection means the law must treat all people alike. Together, the rights to due process and to equal protection guarantee the right to equal opportunity. In other words, it is illegal to treat people unfairly because of race, religion, sex, age, or background.

The Equal Opportunity Laws

People are often the victims of **discrimination**. At different times, people such as African Americans, Latinos, and people with **physical disabilities** have all been discriminated against by certain laws. Women have also been discriminated against. Many people have faced discrimination in jobs and in other areas for many years.

The Fourteenth Amendment says that the states may not deny the people their constitutional rights. It also says that all state and local laws must protect those rights, too. Federal laws, such as the Civil Rights Acts of 1964 and 1968, have been passed to prohibit discrimination. These acts make discrimination in housing, education, and jobs against the law. State and local laws support the federal laws.

Government Fact

You may wish to remember the idea like this: Fourteenth Amendment—Due process + equal protection = equal opportunity.

The laws do *not* say that everyone must be treated exactly the same way in every case. The laws *do* say that no one can be treated unfairly. Suppose a man with only one arm wants a job that honestly takes two arms to do. The company can turn him down for that job because of his physical disability. Suppose the job can be done as well with one arm as with two. Then the man must have an equal opportunity to get that job.

Areas of Equal Opportunity

Housing Much discrimination has occurred in the area of housing. Some owners of houses and apartment buildings would not sell or rent to a person because of his or her race, sex, background, or other difference. Since the Constitution only covered the acts of government, private owners of housing were not bound by the Constitution or its amendments. The Civil Rights Acts changed things. Now, such acts of discrimination are against the law. People may not refuse to rent or sell housing to a person because of race, sex, background, or other difference. These laws give all people the right to go to court to stop discrimination.

Education The Constitution does not guarantee people the right to an education. However, every state has public schools and laws that say young people must go to school. The Fourteenth Amendment guarantees everyone an equal chance to use the public schools.

At one time, "separate but equal" schools were allowed by the government. However, in 1954, the Supreme Court decided that the state laws that permitted segregation were unconstitutional. Keeping students of one race apart from another took away their rights to equal opportunity to education.

Remember
Turn back to Chapter 9 to review the historic 1954 Supreme Court ruling.

In recent years, women have made many gains in employment opportunities. However, their earnings are often still not equal to men who perform the same work.

Today, public schools must give all students an equal chance to get a good education. The courts can force public schools to change when they discriminate against some students. In addition, the 1964 Civil Rights Act says that the federal government can stop sending money to any school that discriminates.

Jobs Some workers often still make less money than other workers doing the same work. Furthermore, women have been discriminated against in the area of jobs for years. They have been shut out from certain kinds of jobs altogether. They have almost always been paid less than men, even when they performed the same work.

The Fourteenth Amendment helps stop such discrimination in jobs. However, it can be used only against federal and state governments. It has no direct power over jobs in private businesses. Some federal laws, such as the Equal Pay Act of 1963, help to solve this problem. Under these laws, any company that gets money from the government cannot discriminate. Many states also have laws that make job discrimination by *any* company illegal.

In 1972, women fought for better protection in jobs and other areas through a constitutional amendment. Called the Equal Rights Amendment (ERA), it was designed to guarantee equal rights to women in all areas. By 1982, the cause for making the ERA an amendment was lost. It fell three states short of being ratified.

✓ Check Your Understanding

1. Who is Rosa Parks? Why is she important?

2. What does due process mean?

3. In what areas are people often the victims of discrimination?

Citizenship and You

FORMING OPINIONS

To take part in government, you must form opinions. That is, you must know which ideas you believe in. You have the power to take part in government. First, you must decide that there are government problems. Then you should study how the problems can be solved.

Suppose many people in your city begin to organize against people who own apartment buildings. "Rents are too high," they say. "The owners do not need all the money they are charging. Most people do not earn that much money in this town." Someone writes a petition for a law that limits the rent an owner can charge. Many people sign the petition. The city council writes an idea for a law on lower rents.

The apartment owners, of course, do not want such a law. They say they need more, not less, money to pay for keeping up the buildings. "If a law limits rents," they say, "our buildings will become unsafe."

How can you best decide what your opinion is? First, you can gather facts and information. Read the newspaper and listen to the radio. Second, you could talk to people on each side. Third, you could go to the city council meetings. People for both sides will debate the proposed law at the meetings.

1. What are the different solutions to the problem or question? What does each group want?

2. Make a chart of arguments for and against to help you form your own opinion.

LANDMARK CHANGES IN THE LAW
Equal Opportunity

In 1973, Maureen Bullock was training to be a restaurant **manager**. She worked for a restaurant chain in Louisiana. She and a man in the training program received the same pay—$450 a month. Later, they both became restaurant managers for the same company. Bullock's pay was $600 a month. The man's was $750. Three months later, each one received another raise. Her pay was now $720 a month, but his was $800.

Bullock felt that she was being paid less because she was a woman. She decided to take her case to federal court. When Bullock went to court, the restaurant chain fired her.

Bullock's case came to court. She showed that her job required the same skills and had the same responsibilities as the man's. She wanted the same pay as the man because she did the same work.

The restaurant chain pointed out that good managers had to be leaders. It said that Bullock was a woman, so she could not be as good a leader as a man. The restaurant chain paid Bullock less because it felt she was less fit for the job.

The court found that the restaurant chain had discriminated against Bullock because of her sex. The court pointed out that Bullock had carried out her job well. It also said there was no proof that men made better managers than women.

The court ordered the restaurant chain to pay Bullock the difference between her salary and what she would have made at the man's higher pay. Finally, the court ruled that Bullock could not be fired for standing up for her rights. In the end, Bullock won the right to equal pay for equal work.

You Decide

Should women always receive the same pay as men if they perform the same job? Why or why not?

Summary

The Fourteenth Amendment guarantees due process and equal protection under the law. Together, these ideas have come to mean that all people are guaranteed equal opportunity. Equal opportunity laws protect people against discrimination.

The Fourteenth Amendment says that the states may not deny people their constitutional rights. Federal laws have made discrimination in housing, education, and jobs against the law.

There are three main areas in which the laws protect the people's right to equal opportunity: housing, education, and jobs.

Vocabulary Review

Write *true* or *false*. If the statement is false, change the underlined term to make it true.

1. A <u>manager</u> is in charge of other workers.

2. To treat two people equally under the law is an example of <u>equal opportunity</u>.

3. The way the bus driver treated Rosa Parks is an example of <u>discrimination</u>.

4. <u>Due process</u> helps to protect people who are treated unfairly.

5. <u>Equal protection</u> guarantees that every citizen has the same chances in life.

Chapter Quiz

Write your answers in complete sentences.

1. What did the Supreme Court decide in the Rosa Parks case?

2. What does *due process* mean?

3. What other part of the Fourteenth Amendment combines with due process to give the people equal opportunity?

4. What laws passed during the 1960s made discrimination illegal in areas such as housing, education, and jobs?

5. What did the Supreme Court decide in 1954 with regard to education in public schools?

6. What did the federal court decide in the job discrimination case of Maureen Bullock?

7. Critical Thinking Give one example each of job and housing discrimination.

8. Critical Thinking How does the Civil Rights Act of 1964 help fight discrimination in public schools?

Write About Government

Complete the following activity.

You have read about discrimination in housing, in education, and in jobs. Create a flyer or a bumper sticker that protests one of these forms of discrimination.

Chapter ▶ 21 ▶ Right to Privacy

Electronic methods of invading people's privacy by "bugging" their homes or offices have been widely developed. Here, listening devices are built into ordinary looking briefcases.

Learning Objectives

- Explain why the right to privacy is important.
- Identify some of the laws concerning the right to privacy.

Words to Know

privacy	the state of not being seen, used, or shared by others
surveillance	a close watch or guard
evidence	facts or information used to prove something in court
warrant	a written order from a judge; a *search warrant* allows police to search someone's house or belongings
welfare	aid, such as money, food, or housing, that the government gives to people who need help

Could This Happen in the United States?

Suppose you come home one day and find that your front door is standing wide open. "Have I been robbed?" you ask yourself. You rush inside to find out what has happened.

Inside, you find the local police slowly searching through all your things. Someone is even reading through all your letters. "You look like a troublemaker to us," one police officer says. "So we're checking to see if you have done anything that is against the law. Just sit in that chair and be quiet until we are done."

Could this happen in the United States? The answer is no—not legally.

In the United States, the Constitution protects citizens against such searches. The Fourth and the Fourteenth Amendments protect a person's **privacy** and his or her property. In most cases, even if the police or the FBI think you have broken a law, they cannot search your home without your permission. They must have a good reason for the search. If you do not agree to a search, it must be approved beforehand by a judge.

Why the Right to Privacy Is Important

Remember
The Fourth Amendment protects people from "unreasonable searches," and the Fourteenth Amendment guarantees "due process of law."

Think back to the time before the United States became an independent nation. Under the king's rule, the king's soldiers could make sudden searches of anyone's home. They could take a person's property without giving a reason for it. The king used these searches to find out who was against his government. He used searches to scare people who might criticize his rule.

When the framers of the Constitution wrote that document, the memory of these searches was in their minds. They knew that freedom from such searches was very important. They thought that such searches were just like stealing. They agreed that people's privacy and property had to be protected by law.

Today, the guarantee of privacy may be even more important than it was then. Today, we have telephones, tape recorders, cameras, and other electronic means of **surveillance**. These machines make spying on people easier than ever before. People must feel that their private lives are protected. They must not be afraid that their homes or offices can be searched at any time by government officials.

There are limits on the right to privacy. The government needs information to catch people who break the law. Even so, the government must follow strict rules in searching someone's house or property. These strict rules help make sure government officials follow the Constitution.

The Right to Privacy Laws

The police, FBI, and other government officials are allowed by law to enter your home. However, they can do so only in a few special cases. First, they can enter and search if you agree of your own free will. No one can search if you do not understand what the search is about. No one can force you to agree to the search. Futhermore, no one can make you afraid of what will happen if you do not agree to the search.

Second, the police can sometimes search your home and take **evidence** without your permission. However, they must have a search **warrant** from a judge. The police do not have to prove to the judge that you have broken the law. They must show the judge that they have a good reason for wanting to search your home. The warrant must say exactly where the police will search. In addition, it must say exactly what the police will search for. If the police do not follow these rules, the warrant is illegal.

Third, the police can sometimes enter and search a home without a warrant. This happens in only very special cases in which they have no time to get a warrant from a judge. In most cases, it occurs where some evidence may be about to disappear. The evidence might be gone if the police wait to get a warrant. Later, the police will have to prove that the evidence would have disappeared by the time they got a warrant.

Fourth, the police can sometimes act without a warrant if evidence is in plain view. Police officers cannot search a car while writing up a parking ticket. Suppose they see illegal drugs lying in plain view on the back seat. They can take those drugs for evidence.

What happens if the police conduct an illegal search? Whatever evidence they find cannot be used in court. Only evidence that is gathered legally can be used against someone.

The courts have decided that the Fourth Amendment protects more than just homes. Offices, hotel rooms, public phones, cars, and other places are protected, too. The Fourth Amendment protects people in any place where they normally expect privacy.

The courts have also ruled that the Fourth Amendment covers telephone wiretaps, hidden tape recorders, and cameras. All these modern ways of surveillance are illegal. If the police use these things, they are violating privacy. Therefore, the rules for obtaining warrants apply to using these methods as well.

✔ Check Your Understanding

1. Which two amendments protect a person's right to privacy?

2. Who must approve a police request to search some place?

Government Skills

PROTECTING YOUR RIGHTS

What can you do when you think the government has taken away some of your rights under the Constitution? If you have enough money, you can hire a lawyer. However, suppose you do not have much money. What can you do to stand up for your rights?

One group you can turn to is the American Civil Liberties Union (ACLU). The ACLU is a special interest group that works to protect the rights of all people. It is very difficult for a poor person alone to fight the government. The ACLU writes letters, files law cases, and pays the lawyers to handle such cases.

In addition, many local governments have legal aid offices. Legal aid is a service in which people can hire low-cost law experts and lawyers. These offices are often partly paid for by the local government. This way all people can fight for their rights, if necessary.

LANDMARK CHANGES IN THE LAW
The Welfare Searches Case

In 1962, some government officials in a county in California thought some people who received **welfare** were cheating. The county thought that certain families had lied about the number of people in the family. The bigger the family, the more welfare money they would get. In order to catch cheaters, the county ordered some early morning searches.

The searches began at 6:30 A.M. on a Sunday morning. Two welfare workers went to each home. When someone came to the door, they introduced themselves and asked to be let in. Inside the house, they searched everywhere.

Some people complained. They took their case to court. They said the county had no search warrants and had never asked for any.

The county agreed that it had no warrants and no reason to think most people had been cheating. However, it pointed out, no family had been forced to open its doors to the welfare workers. They had asked to search, and the people had let them in.

A California court did not agree with the county government. The court pointed out that many of the people who were searched had no other money besides welfare. They needed the welfare in order to live. These people would be afraid to say no to the welfare workers. They would be afraid the county could take away their welfare money.

In addition, the county never told the people of their right to refuse the search. Therefore, the court said, these families had not really agreed to the searches of their own free will. The court decided that a legal warrant is needed in such cases. The county, then, had to stop these searches.

You Decide

Do you agree or disagree with the California court's decision? Explain your answer.

Summary

The Fourth and Fourteenth Amendments give you the right to protect your privacy and property in your home and certain other places. In most cases, government officials cannot search a person's home without his or her permission. If permission is not given, the search is usually approved beforehand by a judge.

There are four basic situations in which government officials can search someone's home. (1) Police can search if they are given permission by the person; (2) Police can search if they have a search warrant issued by a judge; (3) Police can search without a warrant if they believe some evidence is about to disappear; (4) Police can search without a warrant if evidence is in plain view.

evidence

surveillance

welfare

warrant

privacy

Vocabulary Review

Write the term from the list that matches the definition below.

1. Permission to search someone's house

2. Facts used to prove a case

3. Government aid

4. Following someone and tracking his or her activities

5. Having things that are kept from others

Chapter Quiz

Write your answers in complete sentences.

1. What historical reasons are there for the right to privacy laws in the United States?

2. What are two modern methods of electronic surveillance?

3. What are the rights of a person who refuses to allow a search of his or her property?

4. What do government officials need to obtain before searching a home without permission?

5. Under what two conditions can police search some place without written approval beforehand?

6. What did a California court rule in the case of the welfare searches?

7. **Critical Thinking** Why did the framers of the Constitution think amendments to protect people's privacy and property were necessary?

8. **Critical Thinking** Why are there some limits on the people's right to privacy?

Write About Government

Complete the following activities.

1. Do you have the right to privacy in school? Are there limits to your privacy in school? Explain your answer.

2. Do you have the right to privacy at home? How is this right different from the right to privacy guaranteed by the Constitution?

Chapter 22

Rights of the Accused

People accused of crimes have certain constitutional rights. Here, a suspect is questioned by the police.

Learning Objectives

- Explain the constitutional protections of the Fifth, Sixth, and Eighth Amendments.

- Explain why the rights of accused persons are important.

- Describe the rights of accused persons during the arrest process.

Words to Know

accused	charged with breaking the law
defend	to answer against the charge of a crime
commit	to do or perform
confess	to admit to breaking a law
suspect	a person who police think might have broken the law
felony	a very serious crime

Protections Under the Fifth, Sixth, and Eighth Amendments

Have you ever seen an arrest take place on a television show? The police come to the door, arrest someone, and take the person to jail.

Suppose one day the police come to *your* door. Someone in your neighborhood was robbed the night before. The robber looked something like you, the officers say. The police want to ask you questions. You did not rob anyone, but you are scared. You feel you must go along with what the police say.

In fact, you were home alone the night before. No one saw you. You did not talk to anyone. No one can back up your story. What if the person who was robbed thinks you are the robber? What can happen to you? What are your rights?

Nothing can protect you from being **accused** of a crime. The Fifth, Sixth, and Eighth Amendments of the U.S. Constitution protect your rights if you are accused. These amendments guarantee you the right to know what the criminal charges are against you. They guarantee you the right to have a lawyer. You also have the right to keep silent about the things you did and the right to have a fair bail set. These rights help give you the best chance to **defend** yourself against any criminal charges.

Why the Rights of the Accused Are Important

In the United States, every accused person has the right to know the charge against him or her. It is important to know this in order for people to prove their innocence. An accused person also has the right to know how, where, and when he or she is supposed to have **committed** the crime.

Accused persons also need to be able to remain silent. They need to be able to have a lawyer. Without these protections, they might say things that make them appear guilty. Innocent people have sometimes been frightened into **confessing** crimes they did not commit. Sometimes, people have been tricked into confessing crimes much worse than robbery.

Accused persons also need the right to a fair bail. Accused people need to be free to gather the proof to show their innocence. Bail is also important so that innocent people do not have to spend too much time in jail.

The Laws About Rights of the Accused

Arrest The police can arrest a **suspect** only if they accuse that person of a crime. They can stop and question anyone without making an arrest. To protect themselves, the police can search someone for dangerous weapons. They can ask anyone for information about a crime. However, they cannot make an arrest unless they follow certain rules. If they *force* someone to go to the police station with them, it is an arrest.

To arrest someone, the police usually need an arrest warrant. To get it, they need a good reason to think a person has broken the law. The warrant must say what law they think has been broken. If there has been a robbery, the warrant must say who has been robbed, and when and where it happened.

Sometimes, the police can arrest a suspect without a warrant. They do not need a warrant if they *see* someone commit a crime. In addition, they do not need a warrant if they have a good reason to think someone has committed a **felony**. A felony is a very serious crime, such as murder.

For lesser crimes, the police must get a warrant. Suppose a police officer *thinks* someone has committed the misdemeanor of trespassing. Unless the police saw the person commit the misdemeanor, the arrest cannot be made without a warrant. The police must follow these rules in making any arrest. Otherwise, the arrest violates the law, and the case will be thrown out of court.

Questioning Suppose someone is arrested for a crime. The police can take the suspect's photo and fingerprints and write up the arrest. Before asking suspects any questions, the police must read them their rights. These rights are spelled out in the *Miranda* rule. They are named after a very famous Supreme Court case of the 1960s, *Miranda* v. *Arizona*.

A Phoenix, Arizona, warehouse worker named Ernesto Miranda was arrested by police on a charge of kidnapping and rape. He was picked out of a lineup ten days after the crime. After two hours of questioning by police, Miranda confessed. Later, he

Remember
Turn to the complete text of the U.S. Constitution in Appendix B In the back of the book on pages 319–350. Review the words of the Fifth, Sixth, and Eighth Amendments.

The Supreme Court decided that Ernesto Miranda (right) had been denied his constitutional rights. As a result, the Court issued historic guidelines on the rights of the accused.

was convicted in court. During the entire questioning period, the police never once told Miranda of his constitutional rights. On an appeal, the Supreme Court overturned his conviction.

The Court further said it would no longer uphold convictions of defendants who had not been given the following information when they were arrested. All accused persons must be:

- Told of their right to remain silent.

- Warned that anything they say can be used against them in court.

- Informed of their right to have a lawyer present during questioning.

- Told that if they cannot afford to hire a lawyer, one will be provided.

- Told that they may bring any police questioning to an end at any time.

The police must read all suspects the *Miranda* warnings at the time of the arrest. Without these warnings, the answers that suspects give to police questions cannot be used in court. In some cases, people have been given no warnings at all after being arrested. All their statements later were thrown out of court. Some of these people were guilty and even confessed to the crimes. Their statements could not be used because they were not informed of their rights. The police had to use other evidence to try to prove those people guilty.

Bail A person accused of a crime has a right to a fair bail, in most cases. Bail money is handed over to the court. The bail acts as a promise that the accused will appear for trial. Once bail has been paid, the accused is released from jail until the trial. If an accused person "jumps bail" (runs away), the bail money is lost.

Bail must be reasonable. Suppose someone is accused of robbery or some other felony. The court might think there is a chance the accused will run away before the trial. The court then can set a very high bail—$100,000 or more. For lesser crimes, the bail is often lower. This is especially true for people who have never before been in trouble with the law. Sometimes, the court can decide not to allow bail. That only happens if the judge believes the accused person is dangerous or is very likely to run away. If bail is denied, the accused person must remain in jail until the trial.

Government Fact

The Supreme Court based its decision in the Miranda case on the guarantees of the Fifth and Sixth Amendments.

✔ **Check Your Understanding**

1. Which amendments protect the rights of a person accused of a crime?

2. What is a felony?

3. Why did the Supreme Court overturn the conviction of Ernesto Miranda?

On the night of January 19, 1960, Manuel Valtierra was shot and killed in Chicago. The police learned that Manuel and his wife Grace had been having violent fights. At 2:30 A.M., the police arrested Grace, her brother Danny Escobedo, and another suspect named Benny DiGerlando. The three were questioned until 5:30 P.M. the next day. Finally, a lawyer got them out of jail by getting a court order.

On January 30, Danny Escobedo was arrested again. He asked for his lawyer. He refused to answer any questions. When the lawyer came to the station, the police refused to let him see Escobedo. For nearly five hours, the lawyer tried to see him. For five hours, the police refused. Finally, the lawyer left.

Escobedo was questioned again and again for hours. There were different stories about what happened during the questioning. Escobedo said one officer promised to let him go home if he made a statement against Benny DiGerlando. Later, the officer said he made no such promise.

What is known is that the police told Escobedo that DiGerlando had accused him of the murder. Later, the police brought both men face to face. Escobedo said to DiGerlando, "I didn't shoot Manuel. You did it." This was a dangerous and harmful statement. The police took it as evidence that Escobedo knew about the murder. Under state law, that would make him a party to the crime, almost as if he had fired the gun himself.

In court, Escobedo's words were used as evidence that he knew about the murder. The jury believed that he had made these statements of his own free will. They believed the police had promised him nothing in return. He was found guilty and sentenced to 20 years in jail. His case went to a higher state court. That court upheld his conviction.

Three years later, Escobedo's case reached the Supreme Court. The Court decided that the investigation had been handled unfairly by the police. When Escobedo was arrested, the police wanted much more than information. They wanted him to confess. Escobedo had asked again and again to see his lawyer. The lawyer had asked to see him. The police had kept them apart.

The Court said all of this was unfair. The Court decided that Escobedo's constitutional rights had been taken away while he was being questioned. The statements he made at that time could not be used as evidence. The evidence was thrown out, and Escobedo's conviction was overturned. He was released from jail.

You Decide

How would you have decided the Escobedo case? Should the Court have ordered his release from jail as it did? Or, should it have just ordered a new trial to be held? Why?

The Supreme Court ruled that Danny Escobedo had been the subject of an unfair police investigation.

Summary

The Fifth, Sixth, and Eighth Amendments to the Constitution protect the rights of persons accused of crimes. These amendments guarantee accused persons the right to a lawyer, the right to keep silent, and the right to a fair bail.

The laws about the rights of the accused apply during the stages of an arrest and questioning by police.

Usually, police need an arrest warrant to make an arrest.

Police must inform all arrested people of their constitutional rights. These rights were spelled out by the Supreme Court in the case, *Miranda* v. *Arizona*.

Accused persons have a right to a reasonable bail. In some serious crimes, bail can be denied by a judge.

suspect

defend

felony

accused

commit

Vocabulary Review

Complete each sentence with a term from the list.

1. To be put in jail, someone must _____ a crime.

2. A _____ in a crime is investigated by the police.

3. When criminals commit a _____ , they receive a harsh sentence.

4. It is the job of some lawyers to _____ people accused of a crime.

5. When people are _____ of a crime, they are charged with breaking the law.

Chapter Quiz

Write your answers in complete sentences.

1. What four rights do the Fifth and Eighth Amendments to the Constitution guarantee anyone accused of a crime?

2. What details of a crime does an accused person have the right to know?

3. What can the police do in relation to a crime without having to get an arrest warrant?

4. Why would the court set a very high bail for an accused person?

5. Who was Ernesto Miranda? Why was his Supreme Court case important to the rights of the accused?

6. What did the Supreme Court decide in the case of Danny Escobedo?

7. Critical Thinking Why do you think a person accused of a crime should be guaranteed certain rights?

8. Critical Thinking Why is it important that suspects be informed of their rights at the time of arrest?

Write About Government

Complete the following activity.

The *Miranda* rule has been required by law for more than 30 years. However, not everyone likes it. Many law enforcement officials in the country say it stops them from catching guilty people. They also say it puts lawbreakers back on the streets too easily.

What do you think? Are the *Miranda* rights fair? Why or why not? Should they be changed or limited in some way? Why or why not?

The Constitution guarantees an accused person a trial by jury.

Learning Objectives

- Explain how the Constitution protects an accused person's right to a fair trial.
- Explain why the right to a jury trial is important.
- Describe the laws relating to fair trials.

#6

Words to Know

prosecution	the case presented to prove that an accused person is guilty; also, the name for the government lawyers who present the case
defense	the case presented to defend an accused person in court; also, the name for the lawyers who present the case; a *defendant* is a person on trial
expert	someone who has a great deal of knowledge in a certain area
impartial	fair-minded; free from prejudice
verdict	the decision of the jury at the end of a trial
juvenile	usually someone who is under 18 years old

Constitutional Protection for a Fair Trial

You have been arrested for robbery. Now your trial is starting. You are in a courtroom full of people. You see the 12 members of the jury sitting in the jury box. No one is smiling. The lawyers for the **prosecution** will try to prove that you are guilty. Their pieces of evidence are in front of them. The judge is looking down at you. Everyone in the courtroom is waiting for your lawyer to present the **defense** case.

You know you are innocent. Yet, what chance do you have? The police have detectives and scientists who have gathered evidence to use against you. The prosecution lawyers are very smart. They know many ways of proving that accused people are guilty. All these people are **experts**. You have never been in a courtroom before. How can you possibly get a fair trial? The U.S. Constitution can help you get one.

The rights of accused people are so important that the Constitution has four amendments that list these rights. The Fifth, Sixth, Eighth, and Fourteenth Amendments to the Constitution help accused people get a fair trial. Among other things, these amendments promise you the following:

- Protection against spending needless time in jail waiting for a trial.

- Protection against secret trials. Your trial must be <u>public</u>.

- You may have your own lawyer to defend you even if you cannot pay for one yourself.

- Both the defense and the prosecution must follow the rules for a fair trial.

- You can appeal to a higher court if you think your trial has been unfair.

Why the Right to a Jury Trial Is Important

When people are sent to jail, they lose their freedom and most of their rights. Sometimes, people are accused of crimes they did not commit. In the United States, people are innocent until they are proven guilty. The Constitution has established ways to protect innocent people. These ways help the truth to come out at trials. Having a jury decide the case is only one of these ways.

In a trial, the prosecution tries to prove that the accused person is guilty. The defense tries to prove that the accused is innocent. The framers of the Constitution knew that it often takes a public trial to discover all the facts and learn the truth. The prosecution usually has many experts—police, detectives, scientists, and lawyers. The defense may have its own experts. Therefore, a fair trial depends on several things.

1. The defense is entitled to know the charges against the accused.

2. The defense is entitled to know what evidence the government is planning to use against the accused. This way, the defense can bring in its own experts. It can make as strong a case as possible in favor of innocence.

3. Both the defense and the prosecution must follow the same rules of law.

4. The people of the jury must be **impartial** to insure that the accused gets a fair trial.

Suppose the Constitution did not guarantee everyone a fair trial by jury. Suppose the government could put any suspect in jail any time it wished. Suppose it could leave a suspect in jail for years waiting for a trial. If those things happened, *all* people would lose their rights and freedoms.

The Fair Trial Laws

The Fifth, Sixth, Eighth, and Fourteenth Amendments to the Constitution lay the groundwork for fair trials. The Supreme Court and the state high courts have built on that groundwork.

The following laws come from the Constitution and from what state and federal cases decided about the right to a fair trial.

Before the Trial A jury trial is guaranteed by the Sixth and Fourteenth Amendments. For any crime that can result in a jail sentence of six months or more, a defendant may have a jury. The trial must be speedy and public. Every state has laws that say how soon a trial must be held. Accused persons are protected against spending too much time in jail awaiting trial. Most states have to bring an accused

Government *Fact*

These are just a few of the laws on trials, evidence, and rights of accused people.

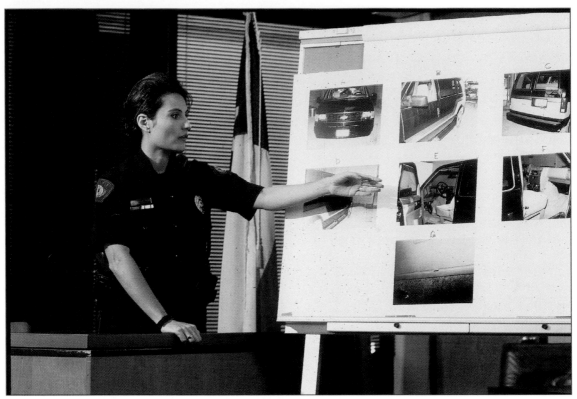

Witnesses help bring out all the facts during a trial.

person to trial within 30 to 60 days of the arrest. The accused may ask for more time if the defense needs it to gather evidence to prove its case.

All parts of a trial must be open to the public. One of the best ways to guarantee a fair trial is to have many people watching. In a few cases, the judge can order a private trial. A trial that involves young children may be heard in private.

The accused has the right to a lawyer for all important parts of the case. Accused persons have to appear at hearings before the trial. They also appear during questioning by the prosecution and at the trial itself. The defense lawyer is the accused person's expert and is at his or her side through all these hearings.

In a previous chapter, you learned that the state must provide a free lawyer to anyone who cannot afford one. A lawyer must also be provided for the first appeal if one is made.

The members of the prosecution team must inform the accused of the charges. They must tell the defense what evidence they have against the accused. They must tell the defense what witnesses they will present during the trial. An accused person has the right to as many facts as possible to build a strong case for his or her innocence. This right is not spelled out by the Constitution. However, it is the law in all federal cases and in most states.

In some cases, a defendant may have the trial moved to another county in the state. Usually, a trial is held in the place where the crime was committed. Suppose the local television and newspapers reported many stories about the crime. The local people may begin to feel that the accused is guilty before the trial even begins. It may be impossible to get a fair trial if everyone thinks the defendant is already guilty. The law says defendants have the right to have the trial moved to another county. In that county, there would be a better chance of receiving a fair trial.

Government Fact

When a case is moved to another county, that is called a *change of venue*.

✓ Check Your Understanding

1. Which amendments to the Constitution help guarantee the right to a fair jury trial?

2. What information must the prosecution supply to the defense before a trial?

3. How are accused persons protected against spending too much time in jail?

During the Trial For all serious crimes, defendants are guaranteed a trial by jury. The jury decides whether the accused is guilty or innocent. Twelve people sit on the jury. All of them must agree on the **verdict**. If they cannot agree, a new jury must be chosen. The trial must be heard again. Some states allow smaller juries for lesser crimes. These states allow a majority vote to decide a case involving a lesser crime.

The accused has a right to an impartial jury. The jury is chosen from people in the community. The lawyers for both sides question the people to see whether they will be fair-minded. The lawyers do not pick people who seem to have already made up their minds about the case.

People who are charged with a crime have a right to hear and see all the evidence and witnesses against them. Defendants cannot be accused of a crime and then kept from witnessing their trial. They must be accused and tried in public. Their accusers must answer questions in public from the defense lawyer.

Defendants can call witnesses to help prove their innocence. Sometimes, witnesses do not want to come to court. The judge can order them to appear at court to tell what they know about the case.

The accused has the right to remain silent during the trial. This is guaranteed by the Fifth Amendment. The prosecution cannot force an accused person to be a witness against himself or herself. However, if the accused decides to be a witness, then the prosecution can question him or her.

The accused has a right to expect everyone in the trial to follow the rules of the law. The judge, defense, prosecution, and jury must all follow the law. If they do not, the accused can appeal the decision.

After the Trial If the accused is found guilty, the Eighth Amendment protects him or her from an unfair sentence. The judge or jury has to give a sentence that matches the crime. Less serious crimes have lesser sentences. Serious crimes can have very severe sentences.

A person found guilty has the right to appeal. A higher court will review the case to see if the trial and the decision were fair. There are several higher courts to which a person who has been found guilty can appeal. Some cases can be appealed all the way to the U.S. Supreme Court.

A person who is found guilty has the right to a lawyer for the first appeal. If he or she cannot pay for one, the government will provide one at no cost. After the first appeal, the government is not obligated to provide a lawyer for free.

Remember
The Eighth Amendment says that a guilty person cannot be punished in a "cruel or unusual" way.

During a trial, lawyers for the prosecution and the defense often have discussions with the judge.

LANDMARK CHANGES IN THE LAW
The Rights of Juveniles

In the legal system, people who are not yet adults are called **juveniles**. Juveniles are usually tried in special juvenile courts. These courts often do not have juries. What rights do juveniles have in court?

One day in June 1964, Marjorie Gault of Arizona returned home from work. Her 15-year-old son Gerald was not at home. She learned that he had been arrested and taken to juvenile hall. He and a friend were accused of making obscene phone calls to a neighbor. When Mrs. Gault went to juvenile hall to find her son, she learned his hearing was set for the next day.

At the hearing, Mrs. Gault and Gerald came without a lawyer. No record of the hearing was made. It is unclear whether or not Gerald confessed to the phone calls. Mrs. Gault wanted the complaining neighbor to appear at the hearing. The judge said the neighbor did not have to appear.

Gerald had been in trouble twice before. One time, there had been a case about a missing baseball glove. Another time, Gerald had been found with someone who had stolen a wallet. This time, the judge sent Gerald to the State Industrial School for six years. He would have to stay there until he was 21 years old. For the same crime, an adult would have been sentenced to only two months in jail.

Gerald's parents appealed. First, they took the case to a lower court, then to the Arizona Supreme Court. The Gaults said they had had no time to prepare a defense for their son. No one had told them they had a right to a lawyer. They did not have the chance to question the woman who had complained. No one had told Gerald he had the right to remain silent.

Both Arizona courts turned down the Gaults' case. The courts said that a juvenile hearing was not a trial. The hearing had followed juvenile laws. The laws did not say that the state had to guarantee juveniles the same rights as adults.

The Gaults appealed to the U.S. Supreme Court. The Court decided to hear the appeal. During its hearing, the Supreme Court's justices asked why Gerald's sentence was so long. Arizona's lawyers said that the sentence was not like sending an adult to jail. The State Industrial School was meant to help, not to hurt. One Supreme Court justice answered that it might not be called a jail, but the boy was not allowed to leave the school. The boy had lost his freedom.

In the end, the Supreme Court sided with the Gaults in the case named *In Re Gault* (1967). The Court said that if juveniles can lose their freedom, their rights must then be protected like anyone else's. The Court also said that states must tell all juveniles what crimes they are being charged with. A juvenile charged with a crime has the same rights as an adult. These are the rights to have a lawyer, to remain silent, to hear and question witnesses, to have an official record of the hearing or trial, and to appeal. According to the Court, the Constitution was not written to protect only adults.

You Decide

Should juveniles be guaranteed the same rights as adults? Should a juvenile who is convicted of a very serious crime be sentenced as harshly as an adult would be? Explain.

Summary

The Fifth, Sixth, Eighth, and Fourteenth Amendments to the U.S. Constitution lay the groundwork for fair trials. Over the years, state and federal courts have decided many cases about the rights guaranteed in these amendments.

The fair trial laws focus on three areas: *Before the trial, during the trial,* and *after the trial.* An accused person's trial must be speedy and public. The accused has the right to a lawyer during every part of the trial. The prosecution must inform the accused of the charge and what evidence there is. The accused has the right to a jury trial. The accused has the right to remain silent during the trial. A person convicted of a crime has the right to an appeal.

Vocabulary Review

Write *true* or *false*. If the statement is false, change the underlined term to make it true.

1. Someone who is <u>impartial</u> makes a fair judgment.

2. Lawyers who argue that someone is guilty of a crime are part of the <u>defense</u>.

3. A <u>juvenile</u> is someone who is not yet an adult.

4. <u>Experts</u> provide testimony in a case.

5. The decision of the jury is called the <u>prosecution</u>.

Chapter Quiz

Write your answers in complete sentences.

1. What information is the defense entitled to know in advance?

2. Why is it important for an accused person to know the charges and evidence against him or her?

3. Why may a defendant ask to have the trial moved to another county in the state?

4. Why is it important for accused people to be able to see the witnesses against them in court?

5. What did the U.S. Supreme Court decide in the case of Gerald Gault?

6. Critical Thinking If a person appeals the trial verdict, what might happen in a higher court?

7. Critical Thinking Why is it important for an accused person's trial to be public?

Write About Government

Complete the following activity.

Look through a newspaper for a story about a local or state trial taking place. Then answer the following questions.

1. Who is the accused person in the case? With what crime is he or she charged?

2. What is the name of the prosecuting lawyer in the case? What is the name of the defense lawyer in the case?

3. What are the names of one witness for the prosecution and one witness for the defense? What did the witnesses say in court?

4. What was the verdict? Was the accused found to be innocent or guilty?

Chapter 24

Political Parties and the Right to Vote

Every four years, the nation's two political parties hold their national conventions. Here, Democrats cheer for their candidates.

Learning Objectives

- Explain the ways political parties serve the country.
- Explain the roots of the Democratic and Republican parties.
- Describe the process of electing a President.
- Explain why the right to vote is important.
- Describe the laws on voting rights.

Words to Know

candidate	a person running for government office
nominate	to name someone as a possible candidate for election
convention	a large meeting of a group of people who share common ideas or goals
political party	a group of citizens who share common ideas about the way the government should carry out its work
primary election	a state election held to help select candidates within a party
delegate	a person chosen to represent other party members at a convention
platform	a set of policies that a political party agrees to work for
citizen	a person belonging to or living in a country
naturalized citizen	someone who was not born a citizen but who became one by law
register	to sign up
ballot	a list of people running for government office and a list of choices about new laws
literacy test	a test to see whether a person can read and write

The National Convention—A Giant Party Every Four Years

It is the summer before the national election for President. The huge hall is filled with people. They wear red, white, and blue ribbons. They carry signs with the names of their favorite **candidates**. Thousands of red, white, and blue balloons float near the roof. Bands play, and people cheer.

These people all belong to the Republican political
party. A candidate has just been **nominated** to run for
the office of President of the United States. Television,
radio, and newspaper reporters bring news of the
event to the rest of the nation. This is the Republican
party's biggest meeting, the national **convention**, held
once every four years. It seems like a giant party.

A few weeks later, a Democratic party convention
will take place. It will also nominate a candidate for
President. All the same things will happen. Candidates
will make speeches. Balloons, bands, and ribbons will
fill the convention hall. Democratic delegates from
50 states will carry signs naming their favorite
candidates. People around the nation will watch
and listen to the convention's activities.

The national candidates, one Democrat and one
Republican, will run against each other for the office
of President. From Labor Day in September until
election day, the first Tuesday after the first Monday
in November, the most exciting political race in our
nation will take place.

Republicans, Democrats, and the Two-Party System

In a democracy, there is power in numbers. The
more people there are who work for a new law, the
more likely that the law will be passed. However,
politics is more than just passing laws. It is the work
of getting candidates elected to office. It is joining
with others who want the same things from their
government as you do. It is working together to gain
the support of other citizens for your ideas. For these
reasons, people join **political parties.**

A political party is a group of citizens who think
more or less alike about government. These people
work together to see that government carries out their

ideas. The United States has two main political parties, the Democrats and the Republicans.

Political parties play a great role in the way our government works. They serve the country in at least five important ways.

1. They choose candidates to run for local, state, and federal offices. Each political party puts up candidates.

2. They point out the weaknesses and poor ideas of other political parties and their candidates.

3. They ask the government for new programs and laws.

4. They spread news and information about party ideas. This helps keep people interested in the work of government.

5. They help keep an eye on how elected officials and lawmakers do their jobs. If they do poorly, they might not be nominated or elected again

The Roots of the Republican and Democratic Parties

Today's Republican and Democratic parties have their roots in the Federalist and anti-Federalist groups from our nation's earliest years. The Federalists stood for a strong central government. The anti-Federalists favored strong state's rights and strong protections for the personal freedoms of people. George Washington, the nation's first President, was a Federalist.

The chart on the next page shows when the nation's political parties first gained the presidency. The anti-Federalists first came into power in 1801, with the election of Thomas Jefferson as President.

Remember
In 1787, the Federalists were in favor of the newly written U.S. Constitution. The anti-Federalists were against the Constitution until it included a Bill of Rights.

Development of Political Parties	
1789	Federalists (George Washington)
1801	Anti-Federalists (Thomas Jefferson)
1829	Democrats (Andrew Jackson)
1861	Republicans (Abraham Lincoln)

Later on, they changed their names to the Democratic-Republicans. In 1829, Andrew Jackson left the Jefferson party and started the Democratic party. He claimed the party would better represent the common man. This party was popular among working people and Americans in the newer western states.

In the early 1800s, Federalists became the Whig party. By the 1840s, the Whigs had become bitterly divided over the question of slavery. Whigs who were against slavery formed the Republican party in 1854. Eventually, the Whig party disappeared entirely. The Republicans first came to power in 1861, when their candidate, Abraham Lincoln, became President. Since that time, the Republicans and Democrats have been the two major political parties in the country.

Electing a President

Remember
In the United States, elections for the President are held every four years.

The most exciting time of work for political parties is during the year of a presidential election. The work starts early in the year, when the party leaders decide whether to run for office. Several candidates may "throw their hats in the ring" for the race to be President. Many states hold **primary elections** in late winter and early spring. Primaries are state elections held to nominate candidates for state and local offices. They are also held to narrow the choices of party candidates for President.

Presidential primaries have become very popular in the last 40 years. There are two kinds. In one, members of a party cast votes for **delegates** pledged to support one particular presidential candidate. If elected, these delegates must vote for that candidate at the convention. In the other kind, delegates are elected to the convention, but they do not have to support one political candidate. States that do not hold primaries hold state party meetings to choose delegates to the convention.

The national conventions take place during summer. A committee at each convention decides on a **platform.** This document is a list of programs and ideas that the party's candidate will support. Each idea on the platform is called a *plank.* The job of the platform committee is to build the platform, plank by plank. The platform is complete when a majority of the members agree on the programs suggested.

The highlight of each convention is the nominating of a presidential candidate. The winners of the different primary elections try to get a majority of delegates to vote for them. The winner becomes the party's candidate for President.

After the convention, the campaign for President begins. The candidates travel to all parts of the country. They meet people, give speeches, debate each other, and in general try to win votes. The news media help keep the race exciting and before the public throughout the campaign. Finally, election day arrives. After the votes are cast, many Americans stay up late at night to watch the election outcome. The winning party celebrates wildly.

The best of all outcomes for a party is when its candidates win both the presidency and a majority of seats in Congress. When the President and the Congress agree, the President can more easily put programs into action. Often, the President and a majority of Congress are from different parties. When this happens, the government continues to work, but the political battles are often fierce.

✓ **Check Your Understanding**

1. Name at least three ways political parties serve the country.

2. Who was the first Republican to be elected President?

Third Parties

The United States basically has a two-party system of government. Democrats and Republicans hold most of the major state and national offices in the country. However, throughout U.S. history, many less powerful political parties have put forth ideas and candidates for office. These parties are called third parties.

Supporters of third parties are often those people who feel that neither the Democrats nor Republicans express their views on government. These third parties nominate candidates for state and national offices just as the Democrats and Republicans do. However, very few third party candidates ever get elected to major political offices. There are several reasons for this.

Third parties are often one-issue parties. That means that a party is formed because the supporters feel strongly about just one issue. Therefore, the party membership remains small, and its appeal is limited. This also usually means that the party will receive very little financial support to push its ideas and its

History Fact

Sometimes, the one issue of a third party is adopted later by one of the two major parties. Child labor laws were once a third party issue.

candidates. In addition, it will be harder for the party to receive TV, radio, and press coverage. All these factors make it very difficult for third parties to play a strong role in the political system.

Third parties have sometimes been spoilers in presidential elections. In 1912, Theodore Roosevelt, who had been President from 1901 to 1909, split from the Republican party. He ran once again for President, this time as a member of the Progressive party. Roosevelt did not win. He actually received more votes than the Republican candidate, President William Howard Taft, who was running for reelection. This result allowed Democrat Woodrow Wilson to be elected.

In 1968, Alabama Governor George Wallace left the Democratic party. He formed the American Independent party and ran for President. Wallace received more than nine million votes, many of them from Democrats. This result allowed Republican Richard Nixon to be elected President with less than 50 percent of the nation's total vote.

In 1912, Theodore Roosevelt ran for President as a third party candidate.

Joining a Political Party

You have to be 18 years old to vote. You can join a political party at any time and work for the ideas that you support. Most of the work of political parties is done by volunteers, people who give of their time without pay. Campaigns are expensive. People are needed to collect donations. Others are needed to fold, stamp, and mail campaign letters. Volunteers walk door to door in every neighborhood, talking to people and trying to win votes for the party's candidates. Many communities have groups of young adults and students who are active party members, such as the Young Republicans or the Young Democrats.

You will have to decide for yourself whether or not you want to join a political party. No one has to join. You can vote whether or not you belong to a party. By joining a political party, you become part of a powerful, large group that actively works for changes. By joining a party, you are likely to keep learning more about government. The more you know about government, the better able you are to decide on candidates and issues at election time.

Who Can Vote?

In the United States, almost everyone 18 years old and over is allowed to vote. However, the sad fact is that almost half of these people do not vote. Why? Some of them say, "Oh, it's too much trouble to vote." Others say, "My vote does not count. It is just one out of millions."

How much is your vote worth? Is it worth fighting for? Is it worth going to jail for?

In 1872, Susan B. Anthony led a group of women to the voting place in Rochester, New York. At that time, women did not have the right to vote in any federal elections. When Anthony and the other women tried to vote, they were arrested. They were tried and found guilty of breaking the law and were fined $100, which Anthony refused to pay.

Anthony and other people kept fighting for a woman's right to vote. For almost 50 years, they marched, petitioned, and protested. Time after time, their leaders were thrown in jail. Finally, in 1920, the Nineteenth Amendment to the Constitution was passed. It gave women the right to vote. Today, the right to vote is promised to every adult American citizen.

The fight for a woman's right to vote reached its peak in the early twentieth century.

Why the Right to Vote Is Important

We live in a representative democracy. We choose the people who represent us in government. The most direct effect you can have on the government is through your power to vote. If you lose your vote, you give up your chance to have a say in government. The same thing happens if you do not use your vote.

Remember
In order to amend the Constitution, a two-thirds majority of Congress has to agree. Then three-fourths of the states must ratify the amendment.

Even more important, if you do not vote, then all your rights are in danger. The Constitution guarantees your rights. However, the Constitution can be changed by your representatives. It could be changed to take away your rights. Of course, such a change is almost impossible to make unless nearly all of the people want it. Still, it could happen, and you choose your representatives by using your vote.

In the past, whole groups of American citizens were denied the right to vote. In fact, at one time over half of all the adults in the United States could not vote! Their lives were run by a government in which they had no say. African Americans and women have gained the vote over the past 140 years. In addition, the voting age has been lowered from 21 to 18 years of age. These groups represented millions of people. When these groups finally got the right to vote, all their problems did not suddenly disappear. However, they now have the power of a voice in government.

The Laws on Voting Rights

When the United States became a nation in 1776, only white adult men who owned land could vote. In 1870, African American adult men got the right to vote. In 1920, women got the right to vote. In 1971, 18-year-olds got the right to vote.

Today in the United States, a person has to meet only four requirements in order to be able to vote. A voter must:

1. **Be a United States citizen** All persons born in the United States are U.S. **citizens.** A person born in a foreign country whose parents are U.S. citizens is also a citizen. People who are not citizens can become **naturalized citizens**. First, however, they must meet certain requirements. They must have lived in the United States for five years and be at least 18 years old. They must be able to read, write, and speak English. They must understand the Constitution and promise to uphold it. They must also take a test about U.S. history and government.

2. **Be at least 18 years old** This age was set by the Twenty-sixth Amendment, passed in 1971. Before that time, 21 was the voting age in most states.

3. **Have lived in the area where they intend to vote for a period of time** Usually, the requirement is 30 days. States have this rule so that only local people can vote in local elections.

4. **Register before voting (in every state except North Dakota)** To **register,** a person gives his or her name, address, age, and other facts to an election official. Then the voter's name is added to the list of other voters in that state. States register voters to keep them from voting twice.

It is against the law for anyone to take away a person's right to vote because of sex, race, background, or religion. A person cannot be stopped from voting because he or she has little money or does not own land. It is also against the law for anyone to use force or threats to stop or change a person's vote.

A person can lose the right to vote in some cases. Most states take away the voting rights of people who have been found guilty of serious crimes. The right to vote can also be taken away from people whose minds are so ill that they cannot care for themselves.

✓ Check Your Understanding

1. What can a person gain by joining a political party?

2. Give two requirements a person needs to be able to vote.

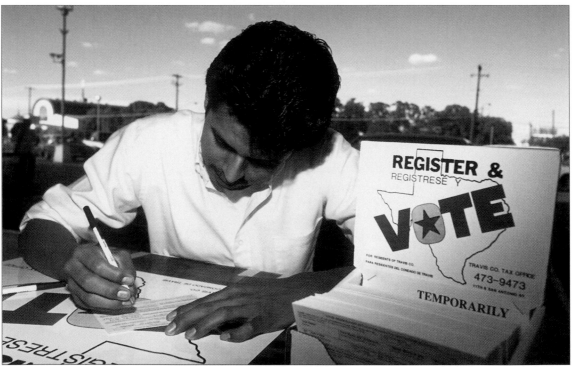

People must register in order to vote in elections. The man in this photo is registering in Texas.

Citizenship and You

PREPARING TO VOTE

Did you know that voting begins before election day? A few weeks before the election, you get a sample **ballot** in the mail. It lists all the people who are running for office in the coming election. It also spells out the new laws and other matters upon which you will be asked to decide.

Before you vote, you should get all the information you can about the candidates and ballot measures. Only then can you decide how to vote. Read newspapers, check the Internet, and listen to the radio and television. They will have news stories about the candidates and the matters on the ballot.

By election day, you should know how you want to vote for everything on the ballot. Mark your choices on the sample ballot. Take it with you to the voting place. This way, you can remember how you decided to vote.

Your sample ballot also tells you when and where to vote. You can vote only at the one place listed on your ballot. In most states, the voting places are open from about 6:00 or 7:00 in the morning to 8:00 or 9.00 at night. If you have to be out of town, you can vote by mail. However, you have to tell the election officials ahead of time.

When you get to the voting place, someone makes sure that you are registered and that you are at the right voting place. Then someone shows you how to vote. In some places, you mark an official ballot by hand. In other places, you use a voting machine to mark your choices. In either case, you vote in private.

After the voting place closes, all the votes are counted. The results of the election are usually made public the next day.

LANDMARK CHANGES IN THE LAW
The Voting Rights Acts

To have any power in government, African Americans and others need representatives who will work for them. They need to vote to get these representatives elected to office. Before they can vote, however, they need to register. In the past, some states did not want African Americans to have any power at all. The white majority in these states tried to keep African Americans from registering to vote.

From about 1870 up through the 1960s, these states often used **literacy tests** to keep African Americans from registering. To register, people had to show that they could read and write. In addition, they had to show they understood the state constitution. All potential new voters had to take the test. The officials who gave the tests sometimes failed African American doctors who took the test. Meanwhile, these same officials passed white sixth-grade dropouts.

The literacy tests were tricks to discriminate against African Americans. Using such tests was legal under those states' laws. Furthermore, the results were frightening. In 1960, for example, there were more than 15,000 possible African American voters in a county in one state. However, only 150 of them had been allowed to register to vote.

In 1965, the federal government passed the Voting Rights Act. This act made the use of literacy tests for registering voters illegal. The Voting Acts of 1968, 1970, and 1975 strengthened these laws.

Several southern states, where literacy tests were most often used, decided to fight against the federal laws. They went to the Supreme Court. They said there was nothing wrong with literacy tests. They said that voters should know as much as possible about the elections they vote in. How can someone who cannot read, write, or understand government be a good voter, they asked?

The lawyers for the federal government had two answers. First, they agreed that a literacy test was not necessarily a bad idea. However, for almost 100 years, literacy tests had been used to keep African Americans from voting. With a history like that, could anyone believe that the results of using literacy tests would suddenly change?

In many places, African Americans had also been cheated out of equal opportunities in education. Because of discrimination in education, African Americans would not have an equal chance to pass a fair literacy test.

The Supreme Court supported the federal government. It said the laws against literacy tests were constitutional. Furthermore, the laws were necessary to fight discrimination. Therefore, in the Voting Rights Act of 1975, the government did away with literacy tests for good.

You Decide

Should literacy tests be allowed? Why or why not?

Summary

Political parties are groups of people who share similar ideas about government and politics.

The United States has a two-party system of government. The main parties are the Democrats and the Republicans.

Many states hold primaries to choose delegates to the national conventions. Other states hold party meetings to choose delegates to the conventions. The convention nominates its candidate for President.

In the United States, a person must meet four requirements for voting. A person must: (1) be a U.S. citizen, or a naturalized citizen; (2) be at least 18 years old; (3) have lived in the area where he or she intends to vote for some time; and (4) register before voting.

platform
primary election
candidate
political parties
naturalized citizen

Vocabulary Review

Write the term from the list that matches each definition below.

1. When states elect candidates to represent each party

2. Someone who was not born in the country in which he or she lives and has citizenship

3. A person for whom citizens vote in an election

4. A set of policies

5. Republicans, Democrats

Chapter Quiz

Write your answers in complete sentences.

1. What are the names of the two major political parties in the United States today?

2. What are presidential primaries?

3. What happens at a national political convention?

4. When did women get the right to vote?

5. Why is it difficult for third parties to gain much public support?

6. Why is the Voting Rights Act of 1965 important in the people's right to vote?

7. Critical Thinking Why do you think the right to vote is important? Give two reasons.

8. Critical Thinking Do you think there should be more than two major political parties in the United States? Explain your answer.

Write About Government

Complete the following activities.

You are in charge of a radio station and television advertising campaign to encourage all eligible citizens to vote.

First, list all the reasons people do not vote.

Then list four strategies you would use to motivate people to vote on election day.

Chapter 25

Responsibilities as a Citizen

Service in the armed forces has always been one responsibility of being a citizen. Today, service is voluntary, but men must still register with the government.

Learning Objectives

- Explain how our rights as Americans bring responsibilities as citizens.
- Describe four responsibilities most citizens have.
- Describe the different kinds of taxes governments collect and what they pay for.

Words to Know

responsibility	something a person must do
census	an official count of the people in a country; also, collected information on their ages, backgrounds, and jobs
tax	money paid to the federal, state, and local governments
income	money that a person earns

Rights Bring Responsibilities

Suppose a young man is accused of robbing the house next door to you. You saw the real robber—an older man—escaping over the back fence. You are afraid that the real robber will come after you if you tell what you saw. The young man on trial has no other witnesses to help him. Do you have to tell what you know?

Suppose you are in charge of hiring a new person for your company. The law says you cannot discriminate against people because of race, sex, or background. You think you work best only with people of your own race and sex. Do you have to give everyone an equal chance to get the job?

The answer to both questions is yes. Under the Constitution, you may have rights and freedoms. However, the laws also give you some **responsibilities**. You take on these responsibilities in exchange for the rights you get. Your right to a fair trial gives you the power to call witnesses to help you win your case. Your responsibility, in turn, is to tell what you know if other people call you as a witness.

You have the right to equal opportunity in getting a job. Therefore, companies have the responsibility to give you an equal chance to get a job. If you are doing the hiring, you must give others an equal chance. Your right to vote gives you the power to be part of your government and help make its decisions. It also gives you the responsibility to follow government decisions once they are made.

These responsibilities do limit your rights and freedoms a little. In turn, everyone's rights are protected, not just your own.

Some Important Responsibilities

Some responsibilities you carry out of your own free will. Voting is one of them. Voting is very important, but no one can force you to do it. The following responsibilities you must carry out, by law, even if you do not want to. These responsibilities have to do with protecting other people's rights as well as your own.

Participate in a trial You may be called upon to play a part in protecting the rights of an accused person. If you get a court order to appear at a trial as a witness, you must appear. When you are called to tell what you know, you must tell the truth. If you do not appear or do not tell the truth, you can be arrested and put in jail.

Remember
To review the details of serving on a jury, turn back to Chapters 16 and 23.

You may also be called to serve on a jury for a trial. The list of possible jurors is taken from registered voters and records of licensed drivers. If you are called for jury duty, you must report. If you have a job, your boss must let you go. You cannot lose your job for serving on a jury.

Register for the armed forces Men 18 years old must register with the Selective Service. This office keeps lists of men who could be called into the armed forces. Right now, the government does not call anyone into the armed forces. Military service is on a voluntary basis. However, the law says that men must register anyway.

Provide information to the government You also have a responsibility to give the government some facts about yourself. The government needs this information to carry out its work. Every day, there are births, deaths, marriages, and other important events. For each event, a paper must be filled out for the government. In addition, every ten years, the federal government takes a **census.** In a census, the government asks questions of everyone in the United States. You are asked about where you live, what you do, your family, your age, your background, and other things. In return for your answers, the government promises to keep your information private.

Pay taxes Everyone has a responsibility to pay **taxes.** Taxes are the money that you pay to federal, state, and local governments. You have no choice about paying taxes. If you do not pay your taxes, you break the law and can be fined or jailed.

Why must you pay? Your federal, state, and local governments guarantee your rights. They protect your safety. They help to keep your neighborhoods clean. They build roads and libraries. They run schools and hospitals. These things help all Americans. However, they cost money. The Constitution gives governments the power to raise the money they need through taxes. You may not always agree with the way government spends the tax money it collects. Your right to vote sometimes gives you the opportunity to say how your tax money is used.

Government Fact

The Bureau of the Census has an Internet Web site. It is a good source of information about the people of the United States.

✓ **Check Your Understanding**

1. Give two reasons why we have responsibilities as citizens.

2. How are our responsibilities an exchange for our rights and freedoms?

Different Taxes and What They Pay For

Income tax The federal government and some state governments charge an **income** tax. This is a yearly tax on the money you earned during that year. The more you earn, the higher the tax. Most people have a certain amount of their earnings taken out of each paycheck. This way, at the end of the year, much of the tax they owe has already been paid to the government.

Money from income taxes pays for most of the federal government's work. It pays for the army, navy, and the operations of all the executive departments. It pays the salaries of the President, the Congress, the Supreme Court justices, and all other federal government workers.

Sales tax The tax you pay most often is sales tax. Most states charge this tax on things you buy. Food is not usually taxed. In most states, the tax is between three and eight cents on every dollar.

The states get most of their money from sales taxes. These funds pay for the state's elected representatives and other state government workers. They pay for schools, highways, dams, and bridges. They also pay for state parks, campgrounds, and all the people who work there. In addition, state taxes pay for safety and health offices, state courts, state police, and most of the other work of state government, including the cost of elections.

You Decide

Do you think your tax dollars are going to good use? Explain your answer.

Property tax Most local governments charge a property tax on land and buildings. The more the property is worth, the higher the tax. Someone who owns a small house pays less than someone who owns two apartment buildings.

Local governments get most of their money from property taxes. These funds pay for local police and firefighters. They also pay for local roads, hospitals, schools, libraries, and parks.

Government Skills

CONDUCTING A CENSUS

Every ten years, the government conducts a census of the population. In recent decades, the census has been conducted largely by mail. The government sends a form with various questions to all the households in the nation. Each household is required to fill out the form truthfully and mail it back.

Read the questions below. They are similar to the questions you would find on a census form. Number a separate sheet of paper from 1 to 10 and answer the questions. When you have completed the form, you will have a census of your household. (You do not have to show any of your answers to your teacher or another classmate.)

1. How many people live in your household?

2. How many adult men live in your household? What are their ages?

3. How many adult women live in your household? What are their ages?

4. How many male children under the age of 18 live in your household? What are their ages?

5. How many female children under the age of 18 live in your household? What are their ages?

6. What is the religion of your family?

7. What is the nationality of your family?

8. What are the occupations of the adults living in your household?

9. Do any of the children under the age of 18 have occupations? What are these occupations?

10. Does your family live in a single housing unit (house) or a multiple family dwelling (apartment building)?

Summary

Under the Constitution, you have many rights and freedoms. The law also gives you some responsibilities.

Some responsibilities you carry out of your own free will. Other responsibilities must be carried out by law.

Governments collect taxes to pay for the work they do. Income tax is the main source of money for the federal government. States get most of their money from state sales taxes. Local governments get most of their money from property taxes. People who own land or buildings must pay property taxes. The local government uses some of this money to pay for things like local hospitals and schools.

census

taxes

responsibility

income

Vocabulary Review

Complete each sentence with a term from the list.

1. Some taxes are based on people's _____.

2. The _____ contains data about the characteristics of a population.

3. The law states that every individual has a _____ to pay taxes.

4. Most states charge _____ on things that you buy.

Chapter Quiz

Write your answers in complete sentences.

1. What is one responsibility you might have at a courtroom trial?

2. What is one responsibility you have if you are hiring a person for a job?

3. What can happen to you if you fail to tell the truth as a witness in a trial?

4. Where does the government get the right to collect taxes from the people?

5. How can you influence the way the government uses the tax money it collects from you?

6. **Critical Thinking** As a citizen, what rights do you have if you are on trial or if you have a job?

7. **Critical Thinking** Why is a census important?

Write About Government

Complete the following activities.

1. What responsibilities do you have as a member of your family? Are these responsibilities voluntary? Can you think of family responsibilities you have that may be required by law?

2. What responsibilities do you have as a student in your school? Are these responsibilities voluntary? Can you think of any responsibilities you have at school that are required by law?

Unit 5 **Review**

Comprehension Check
Complete the sentences by choosing the correct word or phrase.

1. Rosa Parks was an Alabama woman who (fought for a seat on a bus/wanted to run for state political office).

2. Federal laws such as the Civil Rights Act (allow/forbid) discrimination in housing, education, and jobs.

3. Police may search a person's home without a warrant if (criminal evidence is about to disappear/the person is not home).

4. The Fourth Amendment protects people's privacy in (their homes and cars/anyplace they expect privacy).

5. Police can stop and arrest a suspect (only with an arrest warrant/if they see a crime being committed).

6. A judge can deny bail to an accused person if (the judge believes the accused person is dangerous/the accused person has been in jail before).

7. In most states, a guaranteed speedy trial means the trial begins (within six days/within 30 to 60 days).

8. Women in the United States gained the right to vote (when the Nineteenth Amendment became law/when the Voting Rights Act became law).

Writing an Essay
Answer one of the following essay topics.

1. Explain the difference between having rights and having responsibilities.

2. Explain the meaning of the phrase "a two-party system."

3. Summarize the basic rights of an American citizen.

Government in Your Life
Which of the rights that you have as a citizen are most important in your life? Explain.

Glossary

accused charged with breaking the law

administer to manage or have charge of

alliance a union of nations joined in a common cause

ambassador a representative of a government sent to a foreign country

amendment change or correction to a written document

appeal to ask a higher court to review a lower court's decision; *appellate* means having to do with an appeal

arraignment a hearing before a judge during which a person accused of a crime hears the charges against him or her

arrested taken to jail by a law officer

assault an attack on a person by one or more other persons

assemble to gather or meet together; an *assembly* is a gathering of people

assembly a branch of the state legislature in some states

assessor a local official who decides how much tax people must pay on their land, houses, buildings, and other things they own

bail money paid by a person to get out of jail before the trial; bail money pays for a bond, or written promise, that the accused will appear for trial

ballot a list of people running for government office and a list of choices about new laws

bill an idea for a new law that is written and voted on

budget a plan for spending money

bureaucracy a large government organization made up of many offices and bureaus

Cabinet the heads of the executive department of the federal government

candidate a person running for government office

census an official count of the people in a country; also, collected information on their ages, backgrounds, and jobs

ceremonial done in a formal way for a special or important occasion

charter any written statement of right or permissions granted by a ruler or a government

citizen a person belonging to or living in a country

city commission small group of people elected to make laws for a city and run city government; each person on it is also the head of a local department

city council small group of people elected to make laws and run a city's government

city manager a person who works for a city government as the top administrator

civil case involving a disagreement over private rights

civilian not involving the armed forces

colony land owned and governed by another country

commerce any trade or business activity

commit to do or perform

committee a group of representatives and senators in Congress; it meets to study bills, learn about problems in the country, and find ways to solve them

community group a group run by private organizations to help people in need

community services office office that helps people find out what services they can get from county, city, or town government

compromise the making of an agreement in which each side gives up something

confederation an agreement of friendship between states

conference committee a House-Senate committee that works out the differences in bills passed by the two houses of Congress

confess to admit to breaking a law

conservation the act of keeping the natural environment safe and protected

constituents the people who elect a person to public office

constitution a written set of laws, the rules of a government

Constitutional Convention the meeting in 1787 in Philadelphia to write a new plan for a U.S. government

consulate the official home of a *consul*; a consul is a government official sent to a foreign country to protect the home country's business interests and its citizens

contract written agreement between two or more people

convention a large meeting of a group of people who share common ideas or goals

council a group of people who meet regularly to advise the President

county board   a small group of people elected to make laws for and run the government of a county

criminal case   involving a crime, a breaking of the law

criticize   to point out what is wrong with something

customs duty   a government tax on imported goods

deadlocked   a situation in which a jury in a trial cannot reach a decision

debate   to discuss the good and bad points of something

defend   to answer against the charge of a crime

defense   the case presented to defend an accused person in court; also, the name for the lawyers who present the case; a *defendant* is a person on trial

delegate   a person chosen to represent other party members at a convention

democracy   government of a country by its people

dictator   person who has complete power to rule over others

diplomat   a government official who works with governments of other countries

direct democracy   government in which each person in a group votes on all matters

discrimination   the act of treating people unfairly

dissenting opinion   a written statement giving reasons for disagreeing with a Supreme Court ruling

district   a part of a state that elects one state representative or state senator

district attorney   a lawyer who works for the government and brings accused persons to trial

disturbing the peace   to create trouble in a community or neighborhood

divorce   civil court case to end a marriage

due process   the ways laws are carried out to protect people's rights

elect   to choose by voting

embassy   the office and official home of a country's ambassador

enforce   to make someone or something obey a rule or law

environment   the air, water, and land that surrounds us

equal opportunity   receiving the same chance as everyone else to do or have something

equal protection   receiving the same treatment under the laws as everyone else

evidence   facts or information used to prove something in court

executive branch   the part of government that carries out the laws

expert   someone who has a great deal of knowledge in a certain area

export   any product sent from one country or another for purposes of trade

express   to say or show what you think or feel

federal aid   money that the federal government gives to the states; the money helps solve certain problems

federal government   a form of government with two parts, a national government and state governments

felony   a very serious crime

fine   money paid after breaking a local law, such as a traffic law; sometimes, people can pay fines instead of going to jail

floor leader   the leader of each of the two political parties in Congress who directs the debate on proposed bills

foreign policy   the course of action a country takes in relation to another country

government   the control or organization of a country and its people

governor (in the colonies)   someone chosen by the king to rule over a colony

governor   the leader of the executive branch of state government

guilty   judged to have done something wrong or against the law

illegal   against the law

immigration   the act of entering and settling in a country not of one's birth

impartial   fair-minded; free from prejudice

income   money that a person earns

independent agency   a government body or group that is free from control of the three branches of government

information   facts; knowledge given or received

initiative   the process by which the people of a state introduce and vote on proposed laws

innocent   judged not to have done something against the law

intoxicated   drunk

judicial branch   the part of government that rules on what the laws mean

jurisdiction   power or authority

jury   in civil or criminal cases, the people chosen to decide the case

justice court county court that handles criminal cases

juvenile usually someone who is under 18 years old

laws the body of official rules of a country that must be obeyed

legal having to do with the law; acts that are within the law

legislation laws that are made or proposed

legislative branch the part of government that makes the laws

libel to write or broadcast something untrue about someone in order to harm that person

liberty freedom

lieutenant governor the person next in line for the job of governor; takes office if the governor dies, resigns, or is unable to carry out the job

literacy test a test to see whether a person can read and write

local close to home, nearby; having to do with a city, county, town, village, or other small government

majority more than half

majority opinion a written statement giving reasons for a Supreme Court ruling

manager a person whose job is to oversee a group of workers

mayor a person elected as chief executive of a city

misdemeanor a small crime for which the sentence is a fine or less than one year in a local jail

municipal court the name of the local court in most cities

national having to do with a whole nation or country

naturalized citizen someone who was not born a citizen but who became one by law

nominate to name someone as a possible candidate for election

obligation a duty or responsibility

obscene something that offends the public sense of decency

official having the power of the government; an official religion is one set up and run by the government

organize to join in a group in order to work together

overturn to throw out or turn over

patent the official right given to an inventor to make or sell an invention for a certain time without being copied

persecute to harm over and over again; to treat people badly because of their beliefs or ideas

petition   a written notice signed by many people that asks the government to take some action

physical disability   an injury or problem with the body that keeps a person from moving, acting, or working the same as able-bodied people

picket line   a group of people who protest something by marching in front of a building and carrying signs

platform   set of policies that a political party agrees to work for

political   having to do with matters of government

political party   a group of citizens who share common ideas about the way the government should carry out its work

presiding officer   the leader of a government body who runs or directs that body

primary election   a state election held to help select candidates within a party

prior restraint   an order to prevent a person from doing something

privacy   the state of not being seen, used, or shared by others

private   not run by the government

property   the things that someone owns, such as land or buildings

prosecute   to take legal action against someone in court

prosecution   the case presented to prove that an accused person is guilty; also, the name for the government lawyers who present the case

protest   to disagree strongly

public   anything that is run by the government and open to everyone (such as public schools)

recall   a way for the people to remove a state government official from office

referendum   the process by which the people of a state force their legislature to submit proposed bills for voter approval

register   to sign up

regulate   to control by rule or method

religious persecution   unfair treatment of people because of the religion they practice

representative   a person who is chosen to act or speak for others

representatives   members of the House of Representatives

republic   a government by which power is held by representatives elected by the people

reserved   set aside or saved for a special reason

resign   to give up a position

responsibility   something a person must do

review   to look over; to examine once more

riot   an out-of-control fight among many people

secretary of state   the person in state government who keeps state records and runs state elections

segregate   to separate people or groups from each other

senator   a member of the Senate

sentence   punishment set by a court of law for a crime, such as a jail term or fine

session   the meetings of Congress that begin in January each year

slander   to say something untrue about someone in order to do harm to that person

slave   a person who could be bought, sold, and owned by another person

standing committee   House and Senate study group that studies the same problems from year to year

subcommittee   a branch of a standing committee that has a special area of study

superintendent of public instruction   in some states, the person who runs the public schools

supreme   highest

surveillance   a close watch or guard

suspect   a person who police think might have broken the law

tax   money paid to the federal, state, and local governments

term   the length of time a person holds a government office; the President's term is four years

testify   to make statements in hearings or in court to establish one truth or fact

trade   the carrying on of business between states or countries

treaty   an agreement between nations

trespass   to enter or go onto a person's property without permission

trial   a case heard at court before a judge or jury

unconstitutional   a law or government act that goes against the Constitution

Union   the joining of states into one U.S. government

unofficial   having no legal power

uphold   maintain or support

vandalism   the destruction of a person's property

verdict the decision of the jury at the end of a trial

veteran a person who has served in the country's armed forces

veto the power to forbid or stop an act of government

violent showing or acting with strong force that causes harm

voluntary done by a person's own choosing or free will

warrant a written order from a judge; a *search warrant* allows police officers to search someone's house or belongings

welfare aid, such as money, food, or housing, that the government gives to people who need help

whip the assistant to each of the floor leaders of Congress

witness a person who knows or has seen or heard things that are important to a case and is called upon to tell these things in court

The Declaration of Independence

In Congress, July 4, 1776.

The Unanimous Declaration of the Thirteen United States of America

When in the course of human events, it becomes necessary for one people to dissolve the political bands which have connected them with another, and to assume among the powers of the earth, the separate and equal station to which the laws of nature and of nature's God entitle them, a decent respect to the opinions of mankind requires that they should declare the causes which impel them to the separation.

Political Theory of the Declaration

We hold these truths to be self-evident, that all men are created equal, that they are endowed by their Creator with certain unalienable rights, that among these are life, liberty, and the pursuit of happiness. That to secure these rights, governments are instituted among men, deriving their just powers from the consent of the governed. That whenever any form of government becomes destructive of these ends, it is the right of the people to alter or to abolish it, and to institute new government, laying its foundation on such principles and organizing its powers in such form, as to them shall seem most likely to effect their safety and happiness. Prudence, indeed, will dictate that governments long established should not be changed for light and transient causes; and accordingly all experience hath shown, that mankind are more disposed to suffer, while evils are sufferable, than to right themselves by abolishing the forms to which they are accustomed. But when a long train of abuses

Why the Declaration of Independence Was Written
The Declaration of Independence was written because the American colonies decided to break away from Great Britain.

Purposes of Government
The colonists wanted a government that protected the rights of the people. These rights included the rights of life, liberty, and the chance to seek happiness.

and usurpations, pursuing invariably the same object evinces a design to reduce them under absolute despotism, it is their right, it is their duty, to throw off such government, and to provide new guards for their future security.

Grievances Against the King

Such has been the patient sufferance of these colonies; and such is now the necessity which constrains them to alter their former systems of government. The history of the present King of Great Britain is a history of repeated injuries and usurpations, all having direct object the establishment of an absolute tyranny over these states. To prove this, let facts be submitted to a candid world.

He has refused his assent to laws, the most wholesome and necessary for the public good.

He has forbidden his governors to pass laws of immediate and pressing importance, unless suspended in their operation till his assent should be obtained; and when so suspended, he has utterly neglected to attend to them.

He has refused to pass other laws for the accommodation of large districts of people, unless those people would relinquish the right of representation in the legislature, a right inestimable to them and formidable to tyrants only.

He has called together legislative bodies at places unusual, uncomfortable, and distant from the depository of their public records, for the sole purpose of fatiguing them into compliance with his measures.

Reasons for Independence
The Declaration lists reasons why the colonists wanted to be free of the king's government. The people believed this government had denied them their basic human rights.

He has dissolved representative houses repeatedly, for opposing with manly firmness his invasions on the rights of the people.

He has refused for a long time, after such dissolutions, to cause others to be elected; whereby the legislative powers, incapable of annihilation, have returned to the people at large for their exercise; the state remaining in the meantime exposed to all the dangers of invasion from without, and convulsions within.

He has endeavored to prevent the population of these states; for that purpose obstructing the laws for naturalization of foreigners, refusing to pass others to encourage their migrations hither, and raising the conditions of new appropriations of lands.

He has obstructed the administration of justice, by refusing his assent to laws for establishing judiciary powers.

He has made judges dependent on his will alone, for the tenure of their offices, and the amount and payment of their salaries.

He has erected a multitude of new offices, and sent hither swarms of officers to harass our people, and eat out their substance.

He has kept among us, in times of peace, standing armies without the consent of our legislatures.

He has affected to render the military independent of and superior to the civil power.

He has combined with others to subject us to a jurisdiction foreign to our constitution, and unacknowledged by our laws; giving his assent to their acts of pretended legislation:

Charges Against the King
King George III was charged with not letting the colonies have the laws they needed, stopping laws that would set up courts, and making taxes go up.

Charges Against Parliament
The king and Parliament working together were charged with making colonists keep British soldiers in their homes, cutting off colonial trade with other countries, forcing taxes, and not allowing trials by jury in many cases.

For quartering large bodies of armed troops among us;

For protecting them, by a mock trial, from punishment for any murders which they should commit on the inhabitants of these states;

For cutting off our trade with all parts of the world;

For imposing taxes on us without our consent;

For depriving us, in many cases, of the benefits of trial by jury;

For transporting us beyond seas to be tried for pretended offenses;

For abolishing the free system of English laws in a neighboring province, establishing therein an arbitrary government, and enlarging its boundaries so as to render it at once an example and fit instrument for introducing the same absolute rule into these colonies;

For taking away our charters, abolishing our most valuable laws, and altering fundamentally the forms of our governments;

For suspending our own legislatures; and declaring themselves invested with power to legislate for us in all cases whatsoever.

He has abdicated government here, by declaring us out of his protection and waging war against us.

He has plundered our seas, ravaged our coasts, burnt our towns, and destroyed the lives of our people.

He is at this time transporting large armies of foreign mercenaries to complete the works of death, desolation, and tyranny, already begun with circumstances of cruelty and perfidy scarcely paralleled in the most barbarous ages, and totally unworthy the head of a civilized nation.

He has constrained our fellow citizens taken captive on the high seas to bear arms against their country, to become the executioners of their friends and brethren, or to fall themselves by their hands.

He has excited domestic insurrections amongst us, and has endeavored to bring on the inhabitants of our frontiers, the merciless Indian savages, whose known rule of warfare, is an undistinguished destruction of all ages, sexes, and conditions.

In every stage of these oppressions we have petitioned for redress in the most humble terms. Our repeated petitions have been answered only by repeated injury. A prince whose character is thus marked by every act which may define a tyrant is unfit to be the ruler of a free people.

Nor have we been wanting in attentions to our British brethren. We have warned them from time to time of attempts by their legislature to extend an unwarrantable jurisdiction over us. We have reminded them of the circumstances of our emigration and settlement here. We have appealed to their native justice and magnanimity, and we have conjured them by the ties of our common kindred to disavow these usurpations, which would inevitably interrupt our connections and correspondence. They too have been deaf to the voice of justice and of consanguinity. We must, therefore, acquiesce in the necessity, which denounces our separation, and hold them, as we hold the rest of mankind, enemies in war, in peace friends.

Cry for Freedom
The colonists state they are left with no other choice than to become free. They have asked the king and the British people to listen to them. Neither has responded.

Colonists Declare Their Independence
The final paragraph actually proclaims independence. It says that the United States can make war or make peace, make friends with other countries, and do business with other countries.

Signers of the Declaration
The signers of the Declaration of Independence pledged their lives and all they owned to the cause of independence.

A Proclamation of Independence

We, therefore, the representatives of the United States of America, in General Congress, assembled, appealing to the Supreme Judge of the world for the rectitude of our intentions, do, in the name, and by the authority of the good people of these colonies, solemnly publish and declare, that these united colonies are, and of right ought to be free and independent states; that they are absolved from all allegiance to the British Crown, and that all political connection between them and the state of Great Britain, is and ought to be totally dissolved; and that as free and independent states, they have full power to levy war, conclude peace, contract alliances, establish commerce, and to do all other acts and things which independent states may of right do. And for the support of this declaration, with a firm reliance on the protection of Divine Providence, we mutually pledge to each other our lives, our fortunes, and our sacred honor.

Signed by John Hancock of Massachusetts, President of the Congress, and by the fifty-five other Representatives of the thirteen United States of America.

Appendix B
The Constitution of the United States of America

Preamble

We the people of the United States, in order to form a more perfect Union, establish justice, insure domestic tranquility, provide for the common defense, promote the general welfare, and secure the blessings of liberty to ourselves and our posterity, do ordain and establish this Constitution for the United States of America.

Article I

The Legislative Branch

SECTION 1. All legislative powers herein granted shall be vested in a Congress of the United States, which shall consist of a Senate and House of Representatives.

House of Representatives

SECTION 2. (1) The House of Representatives shall be composed of members chosen every second year by the people of the several states, and the electors in each state shall have the qualifications requisite for electors of the most numerous branch of the state legislature.

(2) No person shall be a representative who shall not have attained to the age of twenty-five years, and been seven years a citizen of the United States, and who shall not, when elected, be an inhabitant of that state in which he shall be chosen.

(3) Representatives *[and direct taxes] shall be apportioned among the several states which may be included within this Union, according to their respective numbers, [which shall be determined by adding to the whole number of free persons, including those bound to service for a term of years, and excluding Indians not

* The blue lines indicate portions of the Constitution changed by amendments to the document.

Preamble
This Constitution was written to see that all citizens are treated fairly, to keep the country safe, and to keep people free for all times.

Section 2. (2)
To be a member of the House of Representatives, a person must:
- Be at least 25 years old.
- Be a U.S. citizen for at least seven years.
- Live in the state he or she represents.

taxed, three-fifths of all other persons]. The actual enumeration shall be made within three years after the first meeting of the Congress of the United States, and within every subsequent term of ten years, in such manner as they shall by law direct. The number of representatives shall not exceed one for every thirty thousand, but each state shall have at least one representative; [and until such enumeration shall be made, the state of New Hampshire shall be entitled to choose 3, Massachusetts 8, Rhode Island and Providence Plantations 1, Connecticut 5, New York 6, New Jersey 4, Pennsylvania 8, Delaware 1, Maryland 6, Virginia 10, North Carolina 5, South Carolina 5, and Georgia 3.]

(4) When vacancies happen in the representation from any state, the executive authority thereof shall issue writs of election to fill such vacancies.

(5) The House of Representatives shall choose their speaker and other officers; and shall have the sole power of impeachment.

Senate

SECTION 3. (1) The Senate of the United States shall be composed of two senators from each state, [chosen by the legislature thereof,] for six years; and each senator shall have one vote.

(2) Immediately after they shall be assembled in consequence of the first election, they shall be divided as equally as may be into three classes. [The seats of the senators of the first class shall be vacated at the expiration of the second year, of the second class at the expiration of the fourth year, and of the third class

Section 3. (1)
All states are represented by two senators. Senators serve six-year terms.

at the expiration of the sixth year,] so that one-third may be chosen every second year; [and if vacancies happen by resignation, or otherwise, during the recess of the legislature of any state, the executive thereof may make temporary appointments until the next meeting of the legislature, which shall then fill such vacancies].

(3) No person shall be a senator who shall not have attained to the age of thirty years, and been nine years a citizen of the United States, and who shall not, when elected, be an inhabitant of that state for which he shall be chosen.

(4) The Vice President of the United States shall be president of the Senate, but shall have no vote, unless they be equally divided.

(5) The Senate shall choose their other officers and also a president pro tempore, in the absence of the Vice President, or when he shall exercise the office of President of the United States.

(6) The Senate shall have the sole power to try all impeachments. When sitting for that purpose, they shall be on oath or affirmation. When the President of the United States is tried, the Chief Justice shall preside; and no person shall be convicted without the concurrence of two-thirds of the members present.

(7) Judgment in cases of impeachment shall not extend further than to removal from office, and disqualification to hold and enjoy any office of honor, trust, or profit under the United States; but the party convicted shall nevertheless be liable and subject to indictment, trial, judgment, and punishment, according to law.

Section 3. (4)
The Vice President of the United States is the lead officer in the Senate. However, the Vice President can only vote in case of a tie.

Organization of Congress

SECTION 4. (1) The times, places, and manner of holding elections for senators and representatives, shall be prescribed in each state by the legislature thereof; but the Congress may at any time by law make or alter such regulations, except as to the places of choosing senators.

(2) The Congress shall assemble at least once in every year, [and such meeting shall be on the first Monday in December, unless they shall by law appoint a different day].

SECTION 5. (1) Each house shall be the judge of the elections, returns, and qualifications of its own members, and a majority of each shall constitute a quorum to do business; but a smaller number may adjourn from day to day, and may be authorized to compel the attendance of absent members, in such manner, and under such penalties as each house may provide.

Section 5. (2)
Each house is responsible for making its own rules. Each house must also keep a record of its daily activities.

(2) Each house may determine the rules of its proceedings, punish its members for disorderly behavior, and, with the concurrence of two-thirds, expel a member.

(3) Each house shall keep a journal of its proceedings, and from time to time publish the same, excepting such parts as may in their judgment require secrecy; and the yeas and nays of the members of either house on any question shall, at the desire of one-fifth of those present, be entered on the journal.

(4) Neither house, during the session of Congress, shall, without the consent of the other, adjourn for more than three days, nor to any other place than that in which the two houses shall be sitting.

SECTION 6. (1) The senators and representatives shall receive a compensation for their services, to be ascertained by law, and paid out of the treasury of the United States. They shall in all cases, except treason, felony, and breach of the peace, be privileged from arrest during their attendance at the session of their respective houses, and in going to and returning from the same; and for any speech or debate in either house, they shall not be questioned in any other place.

(2) No senator or representative shall, during the time for which he was elected, be appointed to any civil office under the authority of the United States, which shall have been created, or the emoluments whereof shall have been increased during such time, and no person holding any office under the United States, shall be a member of either house during his continuance in office.

SECTION 7. (1) All bills for raising revenue shall originate in the house of Representatives; but the Senate may propose or concur with amendments as on other bills.

(2) Every bill which shall have passed the House of Representatives and the Senate, shall, before it becomes a law, be presented to the President of the United States; if he approves he shall sign it, but if not he shall return it, with his objections to that house in which it shall have originated, who shall enter the objections at large on their journal, and proceed to reconsider it. If after such reconsideration two-thirds of that house shall agree to pass the bill, it shall be sent, together with the objections, to the other house, by which it shall likewise be reconsidered, and if approved by two-thirds of that house, it shall become a law. But in all such cases the votes of both houses shall be determined by yeas and

Section 6. (1)
Members of Congress are paid by the government. No one in Congress can be punished or questioned for anything they said while Congress is in session.

Section 7.
All tax bills must start in the House of Representatives. Bills have to be passed by both houses of Congress.

nays, and the names of the persons voting for and against the bill shall be entered on the journal of each house respectively. If any bill shall not be returned by the President within ten days (Sundays excepted) after it shall have been presented to him, the same shall be law, in like manner as if he had signed it, unless the Congress by their adjournment prevent its return, in which case it shall not be a law.

(3) Every order, resolution, or vote to which the concurrence of the Senate and House of Representatives may be necessary (except on the question of adjournment) shall be presented to the President of the United States; and before the same shall take effect, shall be approved by him, or being disapproved by him, shall be repassed by two-thirds of the Senate and House of Representatives, according to the rules and limitations prescribed in the case of a bill.

Powers of Congress

Section 8.
The powers and duties of Congress are listed here.

SECTION 8. The Congress shall have power: **(1)** To lay and collect taxes, duties, imposts, and excises, to pay the debts and provide for the common defense and general welfare of the United States; but all duties, imposts, and excises shall be uniform throughout the United States;

(2) To borrow money on the credit of the United States;

(3) To regulate commerce with foreign nations, and among the several states, and with the Indian tribes;

(4) To establish a uniform rule of naturalization, and uniform laws on the subject of bankruptcies throughout the United States;

(5) To coin money, regulate the value thereof, and of foreign coin, and fix the standard of weights and measures;

(6) To provide for the punishment of counterfeiting the securities and current coin of the United States;

(7) To establish post office and post roads;

(8) To promote the progress of science and useful arts, by securing for limited times to authors and inventors the exclusive right to their respective writings and discoveries;

(9) To constitute tribunals inferior to the Supreme Court;

(10) To define and punish piracies and felonies committed on the high seas, and offenses against the law of nations;

(11) To declare war, [grant letters of marque and reprisal,] and make rules concerning captures on land and water;

(12) To raise and support armies, but no appropriation of money to that use shall be for a longer term than two years;

(13) To provide and maintain a navy;

(14) To make rules for the government and regulation of the land and naval forces;

(15) To provide for calling forth the militia to execute the laws of the Union, suppress insurrections, and repel invasions;

(16) To provide for organizing, arming, and disciplining the militia, and for governing such part of them as may be employed in the service of the United States, reserving to the states respectively, the appointment of the officers, and the authority of training the militia according to the discipline prescribed by Congress;

(17) To exercise exclusive legislation in all cases whatsoever, over such district (not exceeding ten miles square) as may, by cession of particular states, and the acceptance of Congress, become the seat of the government of the United States, and to exercise like authority over all places purchased by the consent of the legislature of the state in which the same shall be, for the erection of forts, magazines, arsenals, dockyards, and other needful buildings; and

Section 8. (18)
The Constitution says that Congress has the power to make any laws it needs to carry out the powers listed in Section 8.

(18) To make all laws which shall be necessary and proper for carrying into execution the foregoing powers, and all other powers vested by this Constitution in the government of the United States, or in any department or officer thereof.

Powers Denied to Congress

Section 9.
These are actions that Congress may not take.

SECTION 9. (1) [The migration or importation of such persons as any of the states now existing shall think proper to admit, shall not be prohibited by the Congress prior to the year one thousand eight hundred and eight, but a tax or duty may be imposed on such importation, not exceeding ten dollars for each person.]

(2) The privilege of the writ of habeas corpus shall not be suspended, unless when in cases of rebellion or invasion the public safety may require it.

(3) No bill of attainder or ex post facto law shall be passed.

(4) No capitation, [or other direct,] tax shall be laid, unless in proportion to the census or enumeration herein before directed to be taken.

(5) No tax or duty shall be laid on articles exported from any state,

(6) No preference shall be given by any regulation of commerce or revenue to the ports of one state over those of another; nor shall vessels bound to, or from, one state, be obliged to enter, clear, or pay duties in another.

(7) No money shall be drawn from the treasury, but in consequence of appropriations made by law; and a regular statement and account of the receipts and expenditures of all public money shall be published from time to time.

(8) No title of nobility shall be granted by the United States; and no person holding any office of profit or trust under them, shall, without the consent of the Congress, accept of any present, emolument, office, or title, of any kind whatever, from any king, prince, or foreign state.

Powers Denied to the States

SECTION 10. (1) No state shall enter into any treaty, alliance, or confederation; grant letters of marque and reprisal; coin money; emit bills of credit; make anything but gold and silver coin a tender in payment of debts; pass any bill of attainder, ex post facto law, or law impairing the obligation of contracts, or grant any title of nobility.

(2) No state shall, without the consent of the Congress, lay any imposts or duties on imports or exports, except what may be absolutely necessary for executing its inspection laws; and the net produce of all duties and imposts, laid by any state on imports or

Section 10.
The states cannot:
- Make treaties with other countries.
- Print money.
- Declare war.

exports, shall be for the use of the treasury of the United States; and all such laws shall be subject to the revision and control of the Congress.

(3) No state shall, without the consent of Congress, lay any duty of tonnage, keep troops, or ships of war in time of peace, enter into any agreement or compact with another state, or with a foreign power, or engage in war, unless actually invaded, or in such imminent danger as will not admit of delay.

Article II

The Executive Branch

SECTION 1. (1) The executive power shall be vested in a President of the United States of America. He shall hold his office during the term of four years, and, together with the Vice President, chosen for the same term, be elected, as follows:

(2) Each state shall appoint, in such manner as the legislature thereof may direct, a number of electors, equal to the whole number of senators and representatives to which the state may be entitled in the Congress; but no senator or representative, or person holding an office of trust or profit under the United States, shall be appointed an elector.

(3) [The electors shall meet in their respective states, and vote by ballot for two persons, of whom one at least shall not be an inhabitant of the same state with themselves. And they shall make a list of all the persons voted for, and of the number of votes for each; which list they shall sign and certify, and transmit sealed to the seat of the government of the United States, directed to the president of the Senate. The president of the

Section 1. (1)

The executive branch is made up of the President and the Vice President. They are elected to four-year terms.

Senate shall, in the presence of the Senate and House of Representatives, open all the certificates, and the votes shall them be counted. The person having the greatest number of votes shall be the President, if such number be a majority of the whole number of electors appointed; and if there be more than one who have such majority, and have an equal number of votes, then the House of Representatives shall immediately choose by ballot one of them for President; and if no person have a majority, then from the five highest on the list the said House shall in like manner choose the President. But in choosing the President, the votes shall be taken by states, the representation from each state having one vote; a quorum for this purpose shall consist of a member or members from two-thirds of the states, and a majority of all the states shall be necessary to a choice. In every case, after the choice of the President, the person having the greatest number of votes of the electors shall be the Vice President. But if there should remain two or more who have equal votes, the Senate shall choose from them by ballot the Vice President.]

(4) The Congress may determine the time of choosing the electors, and the day on which they shall give their votes; which day shall be the same throughout the United States.

(5) No person except a natural-born citizen, or a citizen of the United States at the time of the adoption of this Constitution, shall be eligible to the office of President; neither shall any person be eligible to that office who shall not have attained to the age of thirty-five years, and been fourteen years a resident within the United States.

Section 1. (5)
The President must:
- Have been born a citizen of the United States.
- Be at least 35 years old.
- Have been a resident of the United States for at least 14 years.

Section 1. (6)

If the President dies, resigns, or is removed from office, the Vice President becomes President.

(6) [In case of the removal of the President from office, or of his death, resignation, or inability to discharge the powers and duties of the said office, the same shall devolve on the Vice President, and the Congress may by law provide for the case of removal, death, resignation or inability, both of the President and Vice President, declaring what officer shall then act as President, and such officer shall act accordingly, until the disability be removed, or a President shall be elected.]

(7) The President shall, at stated times, receive for his services, a compensation, which shall neither be increased nor diminished during the period for which he shall have been elected, and he shall not receive within that period any other emolument from the United States, or any of them.

(8) Before he enter on the execution of his office, he shall take the following oath or affirmation:—"I do solemnly swear (or affirm) that I will faithfully execute the Office of President of the United States, and will to the best of my Ability, preserve, protect, and defend the Constitution of the United States."

Section 2. (1)

The President is the commander of all the armed forces.

SECTION 2. (1) The President shall be commander in chief of the Army and Navy of the United States, and of the militia of the several states, when called into the actual service of the United States; he may require the opinion, in writing, of the principal officer in each of the executive departments, upon any subject relating to the duties of their respective offices, and he shall have power to grant reprieves and pardons for offenses against the United States, except in cases of impeachment.

(2) He shall have power, by and with the advice and consent of the Senate, to make treaties, provided two-

thirds of the senators present concur; and he shall nominate, and by and with the advice and consent of the Senate, shall appoint ambassadors, other public ministers and consuls, judges of the Supreme Court, and all other officers of the United States, whose appointments are not herein otherwise provided for, and which shall be established by law; but the Congress may by law vest the appointment of such inferior officers, as they think proper, in the President alone, in the courts of law, or in the heads of departments.

(3) The President shall have power to fill up all vacancies that may happen during the recess of the Senate, by granting commissions which shall expire at the end of their next session.

SECTION 3. He shall from time to time give to the Congress information of the state of the Union, and recommend to their consideration such measures as he shall judge necessary and expedient; he may, on extraordinary occasions, convene both houses, or either of them, and in case of disagreement between them, with respect to the time of adjournment, he may adjourn them to such time as he shall think proper; he shall receive ambassadors and other public ministers; he shall take care that the laws be faithfully executed, and shall commission all the officers of the United States.

SECTION 4. The President, Vice President, and all civil officers of the United States, shall be removed from office on impeachment for, and conviction of, treason, bribery, or other high crimes and misdemeanors.

Section 4.
The President and Vice President can be removed from office by impeachment and conviction by a Senate trial.

Section 1.

The judicial branch is made up of the Supreme Court and lower courts. The Supreme Court is the highest court in the land.

Section 2. (2)

The Supreme Court hears cases involving foreign ministers and state governments. The Supreme Court can also decide if it wants to hear appeals of other cases.

Article III

The Judicial Branch

SECTION 1. The judicial power of the United States shall be vested in one Supreme Court, and in such inferior courts as the Congress many from time to time ordain and establish. The judges, both of the Supreme and inferior courts, shall hold their offices during good behavior, and shall, at stated times, receive for their services a compensation, which shall not be diminished during their continuance in office.

SECTION 2. (1) The judicial power shall extend to all cases, in law and equity, arising under this Constitution, the laws of the United States, and treaties made, or which shall be made, under their authority;—to all cases affecting ambassadors, other public ministers and consuls;—to all cases of admiralty and maritime jurisdiction;—to controversies to which the United States shall be a party;—to controversies between two or more states; [between a state and citizens of another state;] between citizens of different states;—between citizens of the same state claiming lands under grants of different states, [and between a state, or the citizens thereof, and foreign states, citizens or subjects].

(2) In all cases affecting ambassadors, other public ministers and consuls, and those in which a state shall be party, the Supreme Court shall have original jurisdiction. In all other cases before mentioned, the Supreme Court shall have appellate jurisdiction, both as to law and fact, with such exceptions, and under such regulations as the Congress shall make.

(3) The trial of all crimes, except in cases of impeachment, shall be by jury; and such trial shall be held in the state where the said crimes shall have been committed; but when not committed within any state, the trial shall be at such place or places as the Congress may by law have directed.

SECTION 3. (1) Treason against the United States, shall consist only in levying war against them, or in adhering to their enemies, giving them aid and comfort. No person shall be convicted of treason unless on the testimony of two witnesses to the same overt act, or on confession in open court.

(2) The Congress shall have power to declare the punishment of treason, but no attainder of treason shall work corruption of blood, or forfeiture except during the life of the person attainted.

Article IV
Relations Among States

SECTION 1. Full faith and credit shall be given in each state to the public acts, records, and judicial proceedings of every other state. And the Congress may by general laws prescribe the manner in which such acts, records, and proceedings shall be proved, and the effect thereof.

SECTION 2. (1) The citizens of each state shall be entitled to all privileges and immunities of citizens in the several states.

(2) A person charged in any state with treason, felony, or other crime, who shall flee from justice, and be found in another state, shall on demand of the executive authority of the state from which he fled, be

Section 3.
Treason is the act of making war against the United States or helping its enemies. A person can be convicted of treason by the testimony of two witnesses, or if the person confesses in court.

Sections 1–2.
All states must accept acts, records, and laws of other states. Citizens of each state must have the same rights as citizens of other states when visiting those states.

delivered up, to be removed to the state having jurisdiction of the crime.

(3) [No person held to service or labor in one state, under the laws thereof, escaping into another, shall, in consequence of any law or regulation therein, be discharged from such service or labor, but shall be delivered up on claim of the party to whom such service or labor may be due.]

Federal-State Relations

Sections 3–4.
Congress has the power to admit new states. The United States government will protect all states from enemies.

SECTION 3. (1) New states may be admitted by the Congress into this Union; but no new state shall be formed or erected within the jurisdiction of any other state; nor any state be formed by the junction of two or more states, or parts of states, without the consent of the legislatures of the states concerned as well as of the Congress.

(2) The Congress shall have the power to dispose of and make all needful rules and regulations respecting the territory of other property belonging to the United States; and nothing in this Constitution shall be so construed as to prejudice any claims of the United States, or of any particular state.

SECTION 4. The United States shall guarantee to every state in this Union a republican form of government, and shall protect each of them against invasion; and on application of the legislature, or of the executive (when the legislature cannot be convened), against domestic violence.

Article V

Provisions for Amendments

The Congress, whenever two-thirds of both houses shall deem it necessary, shall propose amendments to this Constitution, or, on the application of the legislatures of two-thirds of the several states, shall call a convention for proposing amendments, which, in either case, shall be valid to all intents and purposes, as part of this Constitution, when ratified by the legislatures of three-fourths of the several states, or by conventions in three-fourths thereof, as the one or the other mode of ratification may be proposed by the Congress; provided [that no amendment which may be made prior to the year one thousand eight hundred and eight shall in any manner affect the first and fourth clauses in the ninth section of the first article; and] that no state, without its consent, shall be deprived of its equal suffrage in the Senate.

Article VI

National Debts

(1) All debts contracted and engagements entered into, before the adoption of this Constitution, shall be as valid against the United States under this Constitution, as under the Confederation.

Supremacy of National Law

(2) This Constitution, and the laws of the United States which shall be made in pursuance thereof, and all treaties made, or which shall be made, under the authority of the United States, shall be the supreme law of the land; and the judges in every state shall be

bound thereby, anything in the constitution or laws of any state to the contrary notwithstanding.

(3) The senators and representatives before mentioned, and the members of the several state legislatures, and all executive and judicial officers, both of the United States and of the several states, shall be bound by oath or affirmation, to support this Constitution; but no religious test shall ever be required as a qualification to any office or public trust under the United States.

Article VII

The Constitution will go into effect after nine of the thirteen states ratify, or adopt, it.

Article VII

Ratification of Constitution

The ratification of the conventions of nine states, shall be sufficient for the establishments of this Constitution between the states so ratifying the same.

Done in convention by the unanimous consent of the states present the seventeenth day of September in the year of our Lord one thousand seven hundred and eighty-seven and of the independence of the United States of America the twelfth. In witness whereof, we have hereunto subscribed our names,

George Washington—President and deputy from Virginia

Attest: William Jackson—Secretary

Delaware
George Read
Gunning Bedford, Jr.
John Dickinson
Richard Bassett
Jacob Broom

Maryland
James McHenry
Daniel of St. Thomas Jenifer
Daniel Carroll

Virginia
John Blair
James Madison, Jr.

North Carolina
William Blount
Richard Dobbs Spaight
Hugh Williamson

South Carolina
John Rutledge
Charles Cotesworth Pinckney
Charles Pinckney
Pierce Butler

Georgia
William Few
Abraham Baldwin

New Hampshire
John Langdon
Nicholas Gilman

Massachusetts
Nathaniel Gorhan
Rufus King

Connecticut
William Samuel Johnson
Roger Sherman

New York
Alexander Hamilton

New Jersey
William Livingston
David Brearley
William Paterson
Jonathan Dayton

Pennsylvania
Benjamin Franklin
Thomas Mifflin
Robert Morris
George Clymer
Thomas FitzSimons
Jared Ingersoll
James Wilson
Gouverneur Morris

Amendments to the Constitution
(The first ten amendments are the Bill of Rights)

Amendment 1 *Freedom of Religion, Speech, and the Press; Rights of Assembly and Petition*

Congress shall make no law respecting an establishment of religion, or prohibiting the free exercise thereof; or abridging the freedom of speech, or of the press; or the right of the people peaceably to assemble, and to petition the government for a redress of grievances.

First Amendment—1791
Congress may not make rules to take away freedom of religion, freedom of speech, freedom of the press, or the right of people to assemble peaceably.

Amendment 2 *Right to Bear Arms*

A well-regulated militia, being necessary to the security of a free state, the right of the people to keep and bear arms shall not be infringed.

Second Amendment—1791
In order to have a prepared military, people have the right to keep and bear arms.

Third Amendment—1791

In peacetime, the government cannot make citizens feed and house soldiers in their homes.

Fourth Amendment—1791

People or their homes may not be searched without a good reason. Search warrants can only be issued if witnesses give good reasons under oath.

Fifth Amendment—1791

Only a grand jury can accuse people of a serious crime. People cannot be forced to give evidence against themselves. People cannot be tried twice for the same crime if found not guilty.

Sixth Amendment—1791

People have the right to a speedy and public trial. They must be told what they are accused of, have the right to a lawyer, and can see and question those who accused them.

Amendment 3 *Housing of Soldiers*

No soldier shall, in time of peace, be quartered in any house, without the consent of the owner; nor in time of war, but in a manner to be prescribed by law.

Amendment 4 *Search and Arrest Warrant*

The right of the people to be secure in their persons, houses, papers, and effects, against unreasonable searches and seizures, shall not be violated; and no warrants shall issue, but upon probable cause, supported by oath or affirmation, and particularly describing the place to be searched, and the persons or things to be seized.

Amendment 5 *Rights in Criminal Cases*

No person shall be held to answer for a capital, or otherwise infamous crime, unless on a presentment or indictment of a grand jury, except in cases arising in the land or naval forces, or in the militia, when in actual service in time of war or public danger; nor shall any person be subject for the same offense to be twice put in jeopardy of life or limb; nor shall be compelled in any criminal case to be a witness against himself; nor be deprived of life, liberty, or property, without due process of law; nor shall private property be taken for public use, without just compensation.

Amendment 6 *Rights to a Fair Trial*

In all criminal prosecutions, the accused shall enjoy the right to a speedy and public trial, by an impartial jury of the state and district wherein the crime shall have been committed, which district shall have been previously ascertained by law, and to be informed of the nature and cause of the accusation; to be confronted with the witnesses against him; to have compulsory process for obtaining witnesses in his favor, and to have the assistance of counsel for his defense.

Amendment 7 *Rights in Civil Cases*

In suits at common law, where the value in controversy shall exceed twenty dollars, the right of trial by jury shall be preserved; and no fact tried by a jury, shall be otherwise re-examined in any court of the United States, than according to the rules of the common law.

Seventh Amendment—1791
Judges cannot overturn the decision of a jury, unless they find that mistakes were made.

Amendment 8 *Bails, Fines, and Punishments*

Excessive bail shall not be required, nor excessive fines imposed, nor cruel and unusual punishments inflicted.

Eighth Amendment—1791
Punishment must not be cruel and unusual.

Amendment 9 *Rights Retained by the People*

The enumeration in the Constitution of certain rights shall not be construed to deny of disparage others retained by the people.

Ninth Amendment—1791
The people may have rights that are not listed in the Constitution.

Amendment 10 *Powers Reserved to the States and the People*

The powers not delegated to the United States by the Constitution, nor prohibited by it to the states, are reserved to the states respectively, or to the people.

Tenth Amendment—1791
States and people have powers not clearly given to the government or denied to the states.

Amendment 11 *Lawsuits Against States*

The judicial power of United States shall not be construed to extend to any suit in law or equity, commenced or prosecuted against one of the United States by citizens of another state, or by citizens or subjects of any foreign state.

Eleventh Amendment—1795
The power of the judicial branch is limited to certain kinds of cases.

Twelfth Amendment—1804

Electors vote for President and Vice President separately.

Amendment 12 *Election of the President and Vice President*

The Electors shall meet in their respective states and vote by ballot for President and Vice President, one of whom, at least, shall not be an inhabitant of the same state with themselves; they shall name in their ballots the person voted for as President, and in distinct ballots the person voted for as Vice President, and they shall make distinct lists of all person voted for as President, and of all persons voted for as Vice President; and of the number of votes for each, which lists they shall sign and certify, and transmit sealed to the seat of the government of the United States, directed to the president of the Senate;—the president of the Senate shall, in the presence of the Senate and House of Representatives, open all certificates and the votes shall then be counted;—the person having the greatest number of votes for President, shall be the President, if such number be a majority of the whole number of electors appointed; and if no person have such majority, then from the persons having the highest numbers not exceeding three on the list of those voted for as President, the House of Representatives shall choose immediately, by ballot, the President. But in choosing the President, the votes shall be taken by states, the representation from each state having one vote; a quorum for this purpose shall consist of a member of members from two-thirds of the states, and a majority of all the states shall be necessary to a choice. [And if the House of Representatives shall not choose a President whenever the right of choice shall devolve upon them, before the fourth day of March next following, then the Vice President shall act as President, as in the case of the death or other constitutional disability of the President.] The person having the greatest number of votes as Vice President, shall be the Vice President, if such number be a majority of the whole number of electors appointed, and if no person have a majority, then from the two highest numbers on the list, the Senate shall choose the Vice President; a quorum for the purpose shall consist of two-thirds of the whole number of senators, and a majority of the whole number shall be necessary to a choice. But no person constitutionally ineligible to the office of President shall be eligible to that of Vice President of the United States.

Amendment 13 *Abolition of Slavery*

SECTION 1. Neither slavery nor involuntary servitude, except as a punishment for crime whereof the party shall have been duly convicted, shall exist within the United States, or any place subject to their jurisdiction.

SECTION 2. Congress shall have power to enforce this article by appropriate legislation.

Thirteenth Amendment—1865
Slavery is forbidden.

Amendment 14 *Rights of Citizens*

SECTION 1. All persons born or naturalized in the United States, and subject to the jurisdiction thereof, are citizens of the United States and of the state wherein they reside. No state shall make or enforce any law which shall abridge the privileges or immunities of citizens of the United States; nor shall any state deprive any person of life, liberty, or property, without due process of law; nor deny to any person within its jurisdiction the equal protection of the laws.

SECTION 2. Representatives shall be apportioned among the several states according to their respective numbers,

Fourteenth Amendment—1868
People born in or granted citizenship in the United States are citizens of the United States and the state they live in. No state can take away their rights as citizens.

counting the whole number of persons in each state, [excluding Indians not taxed]. But when the right to vote at any election for the choice of electors for President and Vice President of the United States, representatives in Congress, the executive and judicial officers of a state, or the members of the legislature thereof, is denied to any of the [male] inhabitants of such state, [being twenty-one years of age,] and citizens of the United States, or in any way abridged, except for participation in rebellion, or other crime, the basis of representation therein shall be reduced in the proportion which the number of such male citizens shall bear to the whole number of [male] citizens [twenty-one years] of age in such state.

SECTION 3. No person shall be a senator or representative in Congress, or elector of President and Vice President, or hold any office, civil or military, under the United States, or under any state, who, having previously taken an oath, as a member of Congress, or as an officer of the United States, or as a member of any state legislature, or as an executive or judicial officer of any state, to support the Constitution of the United States, shall have engaged in insurrection or rebellion against the same, or given aid or comfort to the enemies thereof. But Congress may by a vote of two-thirds of each House, remove such disability.

SECTION 4. The validity of the public debt of the Untied States, authorized by law, including debts incurred for payment of pensions and bounties for services in suppressing insurrection or rebellion, shall not be questioned. But neither the United States or any state shall assume or pay any debt or obligation incurred in aid of insurrection or rebellion against the

United States, [~~or any claim for the loss or emancipation of any slave,~~] but all such debts, obligations, and claims shall be held illegal and void.

SECTION 5. The Congress shall have power to enforce, by appropriate legislation, the provisions of this article.

Amendment 15 *Voting Rights*

SECTION 1. The right of citizens of the United States to vote shall not be denied or abridged by the United States or by any state on account of race, color, or previous condition of servitude.

SECTION 2. The Congress shall have power to enforce this article by appropriate legislation.

Amendment 16 *Income Taxes*

The Congress shall have power to lay and collect taxes on incomes, from whatever source derived, without apportionment among the several states, and without regard to any census or enumeration.

Amendment 17 *Popular Election of Senators*

(1) The Senate of the United States shall be composed of two senators from each state, elected by the people thereof for six years; and each senator shall have one vote. The electors in each state shall have the qualifications requisite for electors of the most numerous branch of the state legislatures.

(2) When vacancies happen in the representation of any state in the Senate, the executive authority of such state shall issue writs of election to fill such vacancies: Provided, That the legislature of any state may empower the executive thereof to make temporary appointments until the people fill the vacancies by election as the legislature may direct.

Fifteenth Amendment— 1870
No one can be denied the right to vote on the basis of race.

Sixteenth Amendment— 1913
Congress is allowed to pass a tax on income.

Seventeenth Amendment—1913
Senators will be elected directly by the people.

(3) [~~This amendment shall not be so construed as to affect the election or term of any senator chosen before it becomes valid as part of the Constitution.~~]

Amendment 18 *Prohibition of Liquor*

~~SECTION 1. After one year from the ratification of this article the manufacture, sale, or transportation of intoxicating liquors within, the importation thereof into, or the exportation thereof from the United States and all territory subject to the jurisdiction thereof for beverage purposes is hereby prohibited.~~

~~SECTION 2. Congress and the several states shall have concurrent power to enforce this article by appropriate legislation.~~

~~SECTION 3. This article shall be inoperative unless it shall have been ratified as an amendment to the Constitution by the legislatures of the several states; as provided in the Constitution, within seven years from the date of the submission hereof to the states by the Congress.~~

Amendment 19 *Women's Suffrage*

SECTION 1. The right of citizens of the United States to vote shall not be denied or abridged by the United States or by any state on account of sex.

SECTION 2. Congress shall have power to enforce this article by appropriate legislation.

Amendment 20 *Terms of the President and Congress*

SECTION 1. The terms of the President and Vice President shall end at noon on the 20th day of January, and the terms of senators and representatives at noon on the third day of January, of the year in which such terms would have ended if this article had not been ratified; and the terms of their successors shall then begin.

Eighteenth Amendment— 1919
Liquor cannot be manufactured or sold in the United States.

Nineteenth Amendment— 1920
Women are given the right to vote.

Twentieth Amendment— 1933
Presidents start their new terms on January 20. Congress starts its new term on January 3.

SECTION 2. The Congress shall assemble at least once in every year, and such meeting shall begin at noon on the third day of January, unless they shall by law appoint a different day.

SECTION 3. If, at the time fixed for the beginning of the term of the President, the President elect shall have died, the Vice President elect shall become President. If a President shall not have been chosen before the time fixed for the beginning of his term, or if the President elect shall have failed to qualify, then the Vice President elect shall act as President until a President shall have qualified; and the Congress may by law provide for the case wherein neither a President elect nor a Vice President elect shall have qualified, declaring who shall then act as President, or the manner in which one who is to act shall be selected, and such person shall act accordingly until a President or Vice President shall have qualified.

SECTION 4. The Congress may by law provide for the case of the death of any of the persons from whom the House of Representatives may choose a President whenever the right of choice shall have devolved upon them, and for the case of the death of any of the persons from whom the Senate may choose a Vice President whenever the right of choice shall have devolved upon them.

SECTION 5. Sections 1 and 2 shall take effect on the 15th day of October following the ratification of this article.

SECTION 6. This article shall be inoperative unless it shall have been ratified as an amendment to the Constitution by the legislatures of three-fourths of the several states within seven years from the date of its submission.

Twenty-first Amendment—1933

This amendment repeals, or cancels, the Eighteenth Amendment.

Amendment 21 *Repeal of 18th Amendment*

SECTION 1. The eighteenth article of amendment to the Constitution of the United States is hereby repealed.

SECTION 2. The transportation or importation into any state, territory, or possession of the United States for delivery or use therein of intoxicating liquors, in violation of the laws thereof, is hereby prohibited.

SECTION 3. This article shall be inoperative unless it shall have been ratified as an amendment to the Constitution by conventions in the several states, as provided in the Constitution, within seven years from the date of the submission hereof to the states by the Congress.

Twenty-second Amendment—1951

A President cannot serve more than two terms.

Amendment 22 *Limitation of Presidential Terms*

SECTION 1. No person shall be elected to the office of President more than twice, and no person who has held the office of President, or acted as President, for more than two years of a term to which some other person was elected President shall be elected to the office of the President more than once. [But this article shall not apply to any person holding the office of President when this article was proposed by the Congress, and shall not prevent any person who may be holding the office of President, or acting as President, during the term within which this article becomes operative from holding the office of President or acting as President during the remainder of such term.]

SECTION 2. [This article shall be inoperative unless it shall have been ratified as an amendment to the Constitution by the legislatures of three-fourths of the several states within seven years form the date of its submission to the states by the Congress.]

Amendment 23 *Presidential Electors in the District of Columbia*

SECTION 1. The district constituting the seat of government of the United States shall appoint in such manner as the Congress may direct: A number of electors of President and Vice President equal to the whole number of senators and representatives in Congress to which the district would be entitled if it were a state, but in no event more than the least populous state; they shall be in addition to those appointed by the states, but they shall be considered, for the purposes of the election of President and Vice President, to be electors appointed by a state; and they shall meet in the district and perform such duties as provided by the twelfth article of amendment.

SECTION 2. The Congress shall have power to enforce this article by appropriate legislation.

Twenty-third Amendment—1961
Residents of Washington, D.C. have the right to vote for President.

Amendment 24 *Poll Taxes*

SECTION 1. The right of citizens of the United States to vote in any primary or other election for President or Vice President, for electors for President or Vice President, or for senator or representative in Congress, shall not be denied or abridged by the United States or any state by reason of failure to pay any poll tax or other tax.

SECTION 2. The Congress shall have the power to enforce this article by appropriate legislation.

Twenty-fourth Amendment—1964
No state can deny a citizen the right to vote because of unpaid poll taxes or any other tax.

Amendment 25 *Presidential Disability and Succession*

SECTION 1. In case of the removal of the President from office or of his death or resignation, the Vice President shall become President.

SECTION 2. Whenever there is a vacancy in the office of the Vice President, the President shall nominate a Vice President who shall take office upon confirmation by a majority vote of both houses of Congress.

SECTION 3. Whenever the President transmits to the president pro tempore of the Senate and the speaker of the House of Representatives his written declaration that he is unable to discharge the powers and duties of his office, and until he transmits to them a written declaration to the contrary, such powers and duties shall be discharged by the Vice President as Acting President.

SECTION 4. Whenever the Vice President and a majority of either the principal officers of the executive departments or of such other body as Congress may by law provide, transmit to the president pro tempore of the Senate and the speaker of the House of Representatives their written declaration that the President is unable to discharge the powers and duties of his office, the Vice President shall immediately assume the powers and duties of the office as Acting President.

Thereafter, when the President transmits to the president pro tempore of the Senate and the speaker of the House of Representatives his written declaration that no inability exists, he shall resume the powers and duties of his office unless the Vice President and a majority of either the principal officers of the executive department or of such other body as Congress may by law provide, transmit within four days to the president pro tempore of the Senate and the speaker of the House of Representatives their written declaration that the President is unable to discharge the powers and duties of his office. Thereupon Congress shall decide the issue, assembling within forty-eight hours for that purpose if not in session. In the Congress, within twenty-one days after receipt of the latter written declaration, or, if Congress is not in session, within twenty-one days after Congress is required to assemble, determines by two-thirds vote of both houses that the President is unable to discharge the powers and duties of his office, the Vice President shall continue to discharge the same as Acting President; otherwise, the President shall resume the powers and duties of his office.

Amendment 26 *Suffrage for 18-Year-Olds*

SECTION 1. The right of citizens of the United States, who are eighteen years of age or older, to vote shall not be denied or abridged by the United States or by any state on account of age.

SECTION 2. The Congress shall have power to enforce this article by appropriate legislation.

Amendment 27 *Congressional Compensation*

No law, varying the compensation for the services of the senators and representatives, shall take effect until an election of representatives shall have intervened.

Twenty-sixth Amendment—1971
Eighteen-year-olds are given the right to vote.

Twenty-seventh Amendment—1992
Laws passed by Congress to increase their salaries do not take effect until after the next election of representatives.

Index

Acknowledgments

The Granger Collection 2; Gjon Mili/LIFE Magazine, Time, Inc. 5; The Granger Collection 9; The Granger Collection 10; The Granger Collection 14; The Granger Collection 17; The Granger Collection 20; The Granger Collection 22; The Granger Collection 28; The Granger Collection 32; The Granger Collection 35; The Granger Collection 36; CORBIS-Bettmann 40; W. Cody, CORBIS 42; Mark Reinstein, The Image Works 56; CORBIS/Bettmann-UPI 59; Crandall, The Image Works 64; James P. Blair, CORBIS 68; Logan Wallace, The Image Works 71; Mickey Krakowski, AP Photo 73; Greg Gibson, AP Photo 75; Porter Gifford, Liaison Agency 82 CORBIS-Bettmann 84; Kaku Kurita, Gamma Liaison 86; Terry Ashe, Time Life 87; Charles Feil, Stock Boston 98; Ralph Alswan-the White House, PhotoEdit 101; Paul Conklin, PhotoEdit 104; CNP/Archive Photos 108; LaTrobe Bornitz, The Picture Cube, Inc. 111; USSC 116; Joe Sohm, The Image Works 121; CORBIS/Bettmann-UPI 125; P. Clifford, Liaison Agency 132; Paul Conklin, PhotoEdit 134; Michael Newman, PhotoEdit 137; Kevin Fleming, CORBIS 139; B. Daemmrich, The Image Works 146; Steve Grayson, Los Angeles Herald Examiner 153; Jim Cole, AP Photo 156; AP/CORBIS 159; James A. Finley, AP 162; William Johnson, Stock Boston 166; Bettmann/CORBIS 173; K. Preuss, The Image Works 176; A. Ramey, Stock Boston 179; B. Daemmrich, The Image Works 182; Mary Kate Denny, PhotoEdit 183; Bob Galbraith, AP 188; Eric Millette, The Picture Cube, Inc. 192; John Neubauer, PhotoEdit 196; Roger Ressmeyer, CORBIS 206; CORBIS/Bettmann-UPI 213; Terry Ashe, Gamma Liaison 216; CORBIS/Bettmann-UPI 223; CORBIS/Bettmann-UPI 226; UPI/Bettmann Archive 238; Eslim Anderson, The Image Works 242; Steve Starr, Stock Boston 248; John Griffin 256; CORBIS/Bettmann-UPI 260; Bettmann/CORBIS 263; John Neubauer, PhotoEdit 266; B. Daemmrich, The Image Works 270; John Neubauer, PhotoEdit 273; Wally McNamee, CORBIS 278; The Granger Collection 285; The Granger Collection 287; B. Daemmrich, The Image Works 290; Stephen Ferry, The Image Works 296.